T0196451

Seeds of Wisdom

FOR COSMETOLOGISTS AND BARBERS

MICHELLE JOHNSON

authorHOUSE®

AuthorHouse™
1663 Liberty Drive
Bloomington, IN 47403
www.authorhouse.com
Phone: 1 (800) 839-8640

Published by AuthorHouse 08/23/2018

ISBN: 978-1-5462-0301-8 (sc)
ISBN: 978-1-5462-0300-1 (hc)
ISBN: 978-1-5462-0299-8 (e)

Library of Congress Control Number: 2017912179

Print information available on the last page.

Any people depicted in stock imagery provided by Thinkstock are models, and such images are being used for illustrative purposes only. Certain stock imagery © Thinkstock.

This book is printed on acid-free paper.

Because of the dynamic nature of the Internet, any web addresses or links contained in this book may have changed since publication and may no longer be valid. The views expressed in this work are solely those of the author and do not necessarily reflect the views of the publisher, and the publisher hereby disclaims any responsibility for them.

All scriptures are taken from King James Version of the Bible.

Man and Woman Concept

Contents

Hairdressing Concept

What Others are saying

First of all, I want to express the joy I feel for God touching Michelle's heart and for letting me be a part of this book. It is a wonderful blessing. I want to share how Michelle was a blessing in my life in the eight and a half years we worked in the salon together. God used her to encourage me to stand on the word of God in my business and personal life and to trust God when I was going through a dry season. I know God gave Michelle the wisdom and knowledge to write this book, because what she wrote was the same words she used to minister to me.

I know this book will bless your life, if you receive and apply the wisdom and knowledge God has given her to be a blessing to your business. It has truly been a blessing to mine. The Word of God says in Prov. 19:8, "He that getteth wisdom loveth his own soul; he that keepeth understanding shall find good."

—Ptosha Black
Cosmetologist

After the first weekend of working with Michelle, it was obvious she had a great love and concern for others. I noticed her cleaning up behind other stylists' clients, and that was different for me. In the salon where I came from, you were responsible and held accountable for your own clients. Michelle has one distinctive trait—her speed. She would get clients in and out, and it seemed like no effort at all.

One day, I decided to ask how she does it, and she excitedly explained how she asks the Lord to anoint her with speed to get her customers out so she can get home to her family. Because of that revelation, I now work only Thursday to Saturday. I thought I had been doing well spending time with my family; but on the days I worked, it was extremely late when I arrived home. Michelle encouraged me to get home earlier. Michelle laughs at me no because I'm running out of the salon. Her love and compassion to see others do well is what has driven her to write this stylist and barber's manual.

This book will certainly be a blessing to you in this profession. I have been blessed to work alongside Michelle and receive firsthand information to help my business be successful. Thanks, Michelle, for your hard work, your joy, and all that you do.

—Jennifer Totten
Friend and coworker

Michelle, keep up the good work! This book has truly been a blessing to me. I can relate to every circumstance that you touched on. Being in the profession for seventeen years, I have been through a lot of changes with clients. Sometimes you just don't understand why or what happened or you just let it stress you out. Through it all, we do as your book says, pray and know that everything will be alright. Michelle, you get a thumbs-up for this book. It is really great! It has inspired me a lot, seriously.

I thank God for urging you to write a book for hairstylists and barbers on how to deal with different situations the proper way, according to God's Word and not our own way. Continue to let the Lord use you, because it is a great thing. You have my blessings.

—Linsey Brown
Master Barber

In this book, Michelle gives practical wisdom that will help transform your outlook in the cosmetology field. Being a stylist of fifteen years, I have gleaned a vast amount of information and practical tips from her wisdom as a stylist and a salon owner. She is faithful and professional in her craft and very efficient in her work ethnics. Michelle is compassionate and a thoughtful woman of God. I have watched her help develop the potential in others that they didn't see in themselves. It has helped to cultivate them to present quality and stylish results. Cosmetology and giving practical wisdom about her calling are areas that God has anointed Michelle in, because she is very passionate and creative in every endeavor of her job as a salon owner.

This book has been a blessing to me in areas I didn't understand or didn't know how to deal with properly. After having read her book, I have now the information given and applied it to my own style of cosmetology. Therefore, I know it will work for you. I pray that this book will meet you where you are in the field, and that it will plant seeds of wisdom to guide you with practical ways of fine-tuning your skills as a stylist.

—LaThazsca Jones
Coworker and Christian Leader

Acknowledgements

First of all, giving all glory and honor to my Lord and Savior, Christ Jesus, I thank you, Father, for your Holy Spirit, who leads and guides me day by day.

Special thanks to my husband, Tony, who encouraged me to be the best Christian wife, mother, and hairstylist I can be. Thanks also for encouraging me to write this manual.

To my dear mother, Peggy Helms, who went home to be with the Lord while I wrote this book, I miss you so much. Thanks for believing in me and supporting me in everything I would say or do. To my mother-in-law, Mary Johnson, and to my family, thanks for all your support and love, especially, my sister, Angela Jones. I am grateful to my prayer partners for praying for me when I couldn't seem to muster up one for myself.

I would like to thank Scot and Sean at Pavo Hair Salon for taking their time to be my mentors and allowing me to experience the atmosphere of your salon, and thanks to those who helped but didn't want to be mentioned.

I am blessed to have Dr. Leo Holt, my pastor and a true spiritual father. Thank you for taking me under your wings and treating me like a daughter. And thanks to the

Grace Christian Fellowship family for supporting me in this endeavor.

A special thanks to every customer that allowed me to style and care for their hair, even when I made mistakes and my attitude was horrible. To the customers who had the courage to walk away, because of you, I began to see my faults.

To Jennifer Totten and Angela Jones who supported me in promoting this book by taking time out of your busy schedules and also for pushing me to go forward when I felt like giving up.

Thanks to Mr. and Mrs. John Searles of the Silk 2 products in Atlanta, Georgia, and the entire Silk 2 team for your love and support in this endeavor. You are all awesome.

Foreword

This book presents a timely and powerful departure from standard and traditional practices. With *God's Word for Cosmetologists and Barbers*, readers will uncover their physical and spiritual potential and avoid the pitfall that so many succumb to. Anyone who takes an interest in their beauty will find powerful inspiration in these pages, in addition to practical strategies that yield marked improvements in style and appearance.

Michelle Johnson gives us the physical and spiritual tools to look and live better than ever. Michelle sees the potential in everyday people that most cannot envision for themselves.

I strongly recommend Michelle's teaching to cosmetologists, barbers, and other beauty professionals looking to increase their insights into beauty and to dramatically improve success with their clients. With this book, Michelle Johnson raises the bar for other books in the field by opening a new way of achieving excellence in beauty through God's way.

—Dr. Leo Holt
Pastor and Founder,
Resurrection Life Ministry

Letter of Exaltation
for Stylists and Barbers

To all stylists and barbers:

I want to take the time to say I commend you for your hard work. I've been in the industry for twenty five years, and I'm still learning and working on myself. I wrote this book, because we, as professionals in this field, don't like to talk about our issues and wonder why we are stressed out. To the stylist that have it all together, keep up the good work; but to those having challenges and willing to admit it, I encourage you to seek change. I felt I was a great stylist, but I have hurt and offended clients. Most weren't intentional—I just hadn't been trained to deal with certain issues and certain personalities. Many people don't come to our salons due to things we and stylist before us have done. We have to change the image of our profession. Most of us are awesome stylists and barbers, but don't take it for granted. Take this from me, customers will leave you and think nothing of it, then talk about you to others.

I applaud you for the hard, long hours; for the times your legs or back ache and you never complained when you miss your family and want to tell the last customers no, but you sacrifice and accept anyway; for the days you come in for a client for a special occasion, especially on your off day; and for giving extra services at times but never receiving a thank you or tip. I commend you for trying to satisfy the client, especially when the hair is in bad shape; for accepting a client knowing you had too many but didn't want to let them down; for not taking a break to eat due to a client having somewhere to be; and for paying your supplier and booth fees in a timely manner and never being shown you are appreciated. I commend you when a family emergency comes up and you have to cancel appointments, but the clients don't seem to care, have an attitude on the phone as if you don't have feelings and don't come back for a while. I honor you for the times you were faithful to a client, and the day you couldn't take them, they leave you with a wounded spirit. To the salon owners that are running a real business (since statistics show that 90% are being run illegally), I commend you. Stay in encouraged and keep a pure heart no matter what happens in your life and business.

Great stylists and barbers, keep up the good work. It's because of you that the stars, millionaires, doctors, actors, scientist, policemen, mothers, dads, nurses, teachers, professional athletes, etc., look great. This is a great industry, and it will get better for us. I don't care about U-tube, facebook. Snapchat or whatever internet option that's out there showing tutorials on how to do hair at home, if you be professional and have great customer service you will make it. Don't listen to all the negativity in the industry, just use the tools in the book and you will be great. There is nothing like going to the salon/barber shop. Keep believing and trusting in God, and you will be a success.

—Michelle Johnson

Proverbs 1:5 A wise man (stylist/barber) shall hear and will increase learning, and a man of understanding shall attain unto wise counsel. Proverbs 4:7 Wisdom is the principle thing; therefore get wisdom and with all thy wisdom get understanding. Exalt her, and she shall promote thee; she shall bring thee to honour, when thou dost embrace her. She (wisdom)shall give to thine head and ornament of grace, a crown of glory shall she deliver to thee. So to be a success in the hair industry do as James 1:5 says If any of you (stylist/barber) lacks wisdom, you should ask God, who gives generously to all without finding fault, and it will be given unto you.

Introduction

Like many stylists, I started doing hair in the kitchen. Before attending school, I worked in a salon as an assistant to a well-known stylist. It was there that I learned a lot of dos and don'ts. After working in the salon and running into problems, I realized a lot of *real* issues that are helpful in operating a successful, professional business are often not dealt with. I attended school and learned the theory of hair, but I missed the business part. Money management, customer service, and people skills were not taught in depth. I would learn those things from experience, long after I was licensed.

After being in this industry for 26 years, I'm still learning and working on myself, and I don't claim to know it all. I just want to help others in this field. Even though I'm a black stylist, I've had the privilege to be around other ethnic groups in a salon environment, so I know everything in this book may not pertain to your salon setup. Maybe you're on commission or on a booth rental, Christian or non-Christian, black or white, Catholic or Buddhist, it doesn't matter. I know we all need encouragement if not help with some area in our profession.

Inspired by the Holy Spirit, I'm writing this manual to help other stylists and barbers avoid some common pit-falls. I must be honest and transparent in order to help you, because whomever the Son of God sets free is free indeed. We are free to deal with issues without getting offended. I wrote this book also because I know deep in my heart, if you apply these principles, your business will be a success and monetary rewards.

God is so awesome that He does things in threes; he gave us the Father, the Son, and the Holy Spirit, and all of them are one. God made us a spirit within a body and a soul, which consists of your will, mind, and emotions. In our professions, he gave us three major parts of a hair strand: the cuticle, cortex, and the medulla. Three types of hair types of hair: fine, medium, and coarse. Our God is so awesome.

Stylists and barbers, be excited that your ministry is to do hair! We have the opportunity to witness to a lot of people. Get excited and stay excited about your profession. Be encouraging to new stylists and tell them that no matter how hard it seems, they can make it. We must start caring about people and not just the money, because when our customers are sick on the inside, it shows on the outside—normally in the hair. We must develop caring attitudes about our shop owners and coworkers. Not slothful in business, fervent in spirit, serving the Lord," (Rom. 12:11). Stylists and barbers, we're getting a bad rap about overbooking, being late, and disrespecting our customers and their time. Just because you're not in a hurry to go home to your family doesn't mean they're not. Realize that you're not just doing hair but running a business.

Many of us enjoy beauty industry but don't enjoy the rewards because of long hours and few real vacations. God is calling us to a higher level. We can't be enslaved to our industry. Our marriages, friendships, and children are being overtaken by the enemy, because we don't give them the quality time they deserve. My personal declaration is that those days are over. Time is something that can't be regained. I attended a seminar for stylists, and it was stated that most stylists and barbers' marriages end in divorce due to the amount of time we spend at the salon.

We must stop being in bondage with the long hours and ask God for wisdom to set our schedules and stick to them. We must trust God that He will supply all our needs when we take time off for special occasions such as birthdays anniversaries, graduations, and vacations. Our customers know we have a life outside the salon, but if we don't stress how important our families are, they won't see them as important either. We must spend our money more wisely and avoid debt. From this day forward, we will cancel every assignment from the devil. As stylists and barbers, we must start seeking first the Kingdom of God and His righteousness (His way of doing things), and all things will be added unto us (Matt. 6:33).

The enemy preys on us in some salons by peddling "hot" goods, and we purchase them. We must put an end to it! God said that a false balance is an abomination to Him (Prov. 11:1). Remember that God's eyes are on the good and the evil (Prov. 15:3). "Treasures of wickedness profit nothing:" (Prov. 10:2).

I lost several good customers because of my attitude and because I felt unappreciated. Customers without appointments call to be "worked in," and if we leave on an emergency or family situation, they are offended. They seem to forget about all the times they canceled and were never charged a cancellation fee. We are to be appreciated, because we are "accepted in the beloved," (Eph. 1:6) and we are to expect good things from the people we deal with. Stylists and barbers, there is something wrong when you can buy nice homes, cars, clothes, etc., but don't buy the supplies and equipment you need for your business. We all may have to borrow at one time or another, but all the time? Something is seriously wrong. It's selfishness to keep all your profit, is usury. Please ask God to help you in this area.

As professionals, we should not operate in pride but in humility and confidence through Christ. Some of our businesses aren't growing, because we have too much pride to say, "Help me, what do you use to get the hair like that? Show me. I don't know how to do that." Instead, we will send the customer away dissatisfied! As God increases in our lives, we should decrease in our flesh (John 3:30). Paul said, "For me to live is Christ, and to die is gain," (Phil. 1:21). I believe Paul is not just talking about physical death, but in this life we must die to gossip, jealousy, hatred, envy, offenses, persecutions, etc.

I wrote this book to confront issues that we hate to talk about. I know so many of us in the salon that cry at night and never have anyone in this profession to truly talk to but God about issues you face day-to-day. Just like doctors, lawyers, teachers, etc., discuss troubling cases to get solutions, we can do the same. We have a great profession, and it's time for us to enjoy it. It is time for integrity and character to return to the church and to this industry. God is calling us to higher level, and it is time for change. It's time out for the fighting and unnecessary arguments that go in some of our salons and barbershops, especially in front of the clients.

Stylist and barbers, I know some of the issues we have to deal with is inherited it from older stylist and barbers in this profession. For example, long hours, gossip, allowing clients to do whatever, not reporting income, just to name a few; but we will not talk about them or make excuses for our behavior, because they could only go as far as the knowledge they had. Let's change our industry for the better.

I pray that male hairstylists and barbers utilize this book as well, because there seems to be as much gossip, jealousy, and confusion among men in this industry. It's time-out for looking down at others, especially at educational seminars and hair shows. It's by the grace of God that you are where you are. Just because someone work as a platform hair artist doesn't mean they have it all together. We all should be in this industry to make money and make our clients look good. Passion for the industry makes a difference. Just wanting to make money won't last. Keep a positive attitude and a pure heart regardless of what you go through and you will be a success.

God spoke to me at the end of 2014 and said, "In order to stay successful in these last days it will be excellent *customer service* not just ability to style." So I thrive on that, and it is working in spite of how others in the industry are complaining and making excuses. I pray that you will utilize this manual on a daily basis to have victory in your business, family, and relationships.

1

Confession for Stylists and Barbers

Heavenly Father, I declare that you are Jehovah Jireh, that you will provide me with the customers, supplies, and everything I need to be a successful stylist or barber. I have more than enough. You said, "He that has clean hands and a pure heart; who has not lifted up his soul umto vanity, nor sworn deceitfully, He shall receive the blessings from the Lord, and righteousness from the God of his salvation." (Ps. 24:44).

I speak life to my family, coworkers, and customers today, for the joy of the Lord is my strength (Neh. 8:10), not people or my circumstances. Lord, "let no corrupt communication proceed out of my mouth, but what is good for necessary edification, that it may impart grace to the hearer," (Eph. 4:29). I will rejoice and be exceedingly glad, because this is the day the Lord has made. I curse every negative word that has been spoken against my clientele, my family, my marriage, my abilities, health, and past failures. I loose customers from the North, South, East, and West. I charge the angels for they hearken to the voice of Your Word (Ps. 103:20) to cause customers to come to me. I know that you have pleasure in the prosperity of your servant. I love you, Lord. Thank you for being my daily bread.

Seeds of Wisdom for Our Character

A character is defined as our moral excellence or reputation. Our character has to be addressed. To me, character is what we do when we think no one is looking. We owe it to God, ourselves, and our customers to be honest, reliable, trustworthy, open to advice, quick to avoid useless chatter, to speak only words of wisdom and knowledge, and to watch the way we live. The enemy would love to destroy your name in this industry. For example, rumor has it that all barbers do is drink, talk filthy, and sleep with coworkers' customers, and that all hairstylists do is gossip, never pay their bills, are lazy, always late, and cheat with their coworkers or clients' mates. Be careful, because God said that "a good name is rather to be chosen than great riches," (Prov. 22:1).

We have to stop saying "I don't care what they think." Our reputation—overall quality or character as seen or judged by people in general—is important, because this is a *people*-business. Are you showing any self-control, love, mercy, joy, peace, patience, goodness, faithfulness, and gentleness? If not, I suggest you look in the mirror.

Here are character flaws that we, as stylists and barbers, need to address in our workplace:

1. Working in a salon without the proper requirements.

2. Lying to customers that you are using superior products when you know you're using the cheapest, most inferior products on the market.
3. Hiding in restrooms to avoid paying the supply representative
4. Overcharging certain customers because you know their lifestyle
5. Handling personal business while working on a client's head
6. Going outside to smoke while your client waits.
7. Putting a product in another label to deceive customers.
8. Not coming to work because you haven't paid rental (Be honest and communicate with your boss).
9. Coming to work looking like a mess, with hair undone, and wearing unprofessional clothing.
10. Teaming up with other stylists to hold dryers and shampoo bowls for your clients as if God doesn't see you (If you overbook, accept it).
11. Having customers waiting for you in cars or in the salon (Come in fifteen minutes early. You should greet them, not them greeting you).
12. Telling a customer you'll take them then leave the salon, or schedule or tell them to come on knowing you got to pick up your children/family or do something else. Schedule them later or another say.
13. Having clients fold your towels and sweeping
14. Misuse or stealing of products and/or equipment purchased by the owner or manager to use on your clients or for your personal use.

15. Use of co workers products and equipment without their permission.
16. Can't wait until client completely dries, pay up, and leave, or telling the customer to leave once they are dry (So unprofessional!).
17. Allowing your product or sales representative to disrupt the services you are providing to your customer.
18. Not adhering to the dress code of your salon or barber shop.
19. Not properly sanitizing equipment between clients.
20. Not using proper telephone etiquette like rude tone and not being kind or respectful to all clients.

Integrity is essential to good character. *Integrity* is the adherence to a code of ethics and values. We, as stylists and barbers as well as those that profess to be Christians, should adhere to God's Word and the board regulations in our state in order to be successful. I must admit, I allowed myself to have a shampoo tech without a license for years with the owner's consent, but it was still wrong. I felt so bad. I knew I must do all things decent and in order (1 Cor. 14:40). God kept me, but he spoke one day and said, "The enemy is coming in, and you know where the door is open. Close it." My tech got a job, and I apologized to my co workers and repented to God for being out of order.

Stylists and barbers, ask God to help you buy the products so you can have integrity by not lying to your customers. For example, you're using a certain product, knowing you're putting something cheap on the client, and not giving them what they're paying for. God sees everything. You may think you're doing well, but I promise you, in your business, it will show up sooner or later. Customers will see other people's hair looking healthier and prettier and realize that it's not because they're not drinking enough water, but because you're not using good products or conditioners.

Stylists and barbers, have integrity by letting a customer know that you will be late or that you are not coming in, rather than to have them come to the salon and find out you're not there. Check your integrity level when you write a bad check to your manager or supply person then take off a week as if you don't owe them. Integrity is telling your coworker a customer called looking for the last person who did her hair even though she forgot her name rather than telling the customer to come on in, and you'll do it, not knowing whether it's your client or not. Integrity is telling the salon owner your client broke something and not wait until she ask what happens, and you get offended because she asked.

We can create seasons in our business, and then we have the audacity to say "It's just a season" or "My clients are leaving." You better get a quick heart-check when client tell you they getting wet or having water in their ears, you snatching on their heads; when they complain that the dryer or water is too hot and you ignore them or say it's part of getting your hair done. It is so cruel, and some of us say we love God. Integrity is taking time to lower the heat, try or prevent them from getting wet, and be gentle and sensitive to others. Go the extra mile. Sometimes life isn't just about you. Clients are spending their money, and they deserve to be treated right.

Stylist and barbers know that you may have great skills and it will get you to the top, but only integrity and character will keep you there. Please meditate on these scriptures and ask the Holy Spirit to help you. Only you and God know the things you do when others aren't looking.

"Hear instruction and be wise, and refuse it not," (Prov. 8:33). Be willing to listen to other stylists and barbers who are willing to help you.

"But Let your communication be Yea. Yea. Nay.nay: for whatsoever is more than these cometh of evil," (Matt. 5:37) In order to avoid confusion, don't tell customers I will or maybe; let your yes be yes and your no, no.

"He that keepeth his mouth keepeth his life; but he that openth wide his lips shall have destruction," (Prov. 13:3)

"Recompense no man evil for evil. Provide things honest in the sight of all men," (Rom. 12:17)

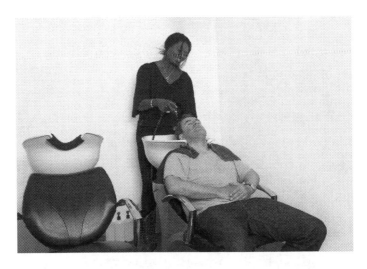

Notes

Things I can do to work on my character and integrity in the industry:

_____

_____

_____

_____

_____

_____

_____

_____

_____

_____

_____

_____

_____

_____

_____

_____

_____

_____

_____

_____

_____

_____

_____

_____

_____

_____

_____

Seeds of Wisdom for Our Attitude

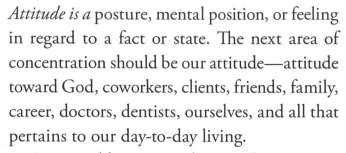

Attitude is a posture, mental position, or feeling in regard to a fact or state. The next area of concentration should be our attitude—attitude toward God, coworkers, clients, friends, family, career, doctors, dentists, ourselves, and all that pertains to our day-to-day living.

I was told at an early age, "You are so pretty, but you have an ugly attitude." I didn't understand what Grandma was talking about until I got older and got filled with the Holy Spirit. Then I saw how ugly I was. I am so excited now to be able to acknowledge my weaknesses and work to improve them. I lost many customers because I had an attitude and thought that I had it all together. But that wasn't true at all. I was rude, in my own slick way, and not a good listener. Thank God for deliverance! I didn't mistreat my clients by coming in late or acting like they don't matter like some of you but since I was good I felt I could say what I wanted for example: A client walks in late I'd said "Excuse you" in front of others instead of telling them in private that if they have to be more than 30 minutes late they will have to reschedule due to my other clients or I will be late getting to them. You can't let what come up just come out and believe the old saying "It's better out than in", that unruly tongue will destroy you and your business. Remember loose lips sink ships (business, customers, booth renters or commission employees). God word tell us life and death is in the power of our tongue and You shall eat the fruit thereof, Proverbs 18:21. Trust me I don't care how great of a stylist or barber you are they will come to their senses that they are spending their money and can be treated better. They would rather be in peace with a stylist that may not be as good as you but she/he is professional. In this, I learned that I still have to be sensitive to others. Spirits attract one another. I've learned that you draw unto you what you really are. If you gossip, you draw gossipers. If you're a complainer, you draw complainers. If your attitude is lazy, you draw lazy people. If your attitude always says "I'm tired," no one wants to be around you. If you're miserable, you draw misery.

If you're happy and laughing, you draw happy and laughing people. So ask yourself, "What am I drawing?" Do you say, "I don't feel like doing hair today" or "I don't feel like dealing with these people," or "My clientele isn't growing," and "I'm making just enough to pay booth fee." If so, I encourage you to change your attitude and see how God moves in your business.

Stylist and barbers, be like David and encourage yourself in the Lord. You can make it and have a great attitude, in spite of what's maybe going on around you. God loves you and want you to be successful. It's true that your attitude determines how far you go in life. Remember, "Man looks at the outer appearance, but God looks at the heart," (1 Sam 16:7). Stop saying, "God knows my heart." Yes, He knows it's ugly! Some of you are awesome stylist and barbers, but your attitudes are horrible. You treat people bad, talk hard, and look down on everyone. Trust me; get it right before you self-destruct. To the seasoned stylist and barbers, you need a heart-check for your attitude to change with new hairstylist. Some of you are so jealous even though you have great clientele, and instead of helping the new stylists, you talk bad about them. Don't forget that you were new to the profession at one time. Remember, what's on the inside shows on the outside. So be positive, no matter what the enemy throws our way. We must realize that the enemy will raise all types of spirits, and God will allow them to perfect something in us—especially if we're Christians. That's why God warned us that "we wrestle not against flesh and blood, but principalities, powers, the rulers of darkness of this world, against spiritual wickedness in high places," (Eph. 6:12).

Stylists and barbers, Paul warned us in Philippians 2:14–25 to "do all things without complaining and disputing that you may become blameless and harmless, children of God without fault in the midst of a perverse generation, among whom you shine as light in the world."

So it's important to work on our attitude, especially in front of the clients. I still ask God to help me keep my attitude right, especially when I can't understand why a lot of us profess to be Christians but won't pick up trash our customers leave behind, won't remove hair in shampoo bowls but leave it for someone else, and won't take time to help lock doors behind clients if needed, just to name a few things. Learn to discuss problems and come up with a resolution. Nothing is perfect—except God. Keep a pleasing attitude. Talk to your clients, learn what they like, give them the style they want not what you want them to have. It's wrong to treat clients bad and they spending their money. So professional I advise you get rid of the nasty, arrogant attitudes just because you are a great stylist/ barber.

Confess these scriptures daily, especially when tests come your way:

> I will not contend with a man (sister or brother) without cause, if he has done me no harm (Prov. 3:30).
>
> I will not have a proud look (one that overestimates himself and underestimates another), because God hates that (Prov. 6:17).
>
> I will humble myself under the mighty hands of God so that in due time, he may exalt me (1 Pet. 5:6).

Words of Wisdom for Our Mouths

As stylists, barbers, and salon owners, we need to watch what we say. I have made many mistakes just by not shutting up, telling the absolute truth no matter who it offended, and being judgmental. I realized after getting in the Word of God and not just in church that what we say is important in determining the way our lives will go. I learned that any man who looks in a mirror and doesn't see himself is deceived. And by getting in the word of God, I began to see myself. I began to see how harsh and rude I was with my speech, and I discovered that due to past hurts, mostly from trying to help others. It was my line of defense and my only way I thought of protecting myself, until I realized I was only hurting my business and others. I had to repent (change). I learned that the truth will set you free once it is acted on. A lot of us know, but are in denial, and until you admit your problems, you will stay in bondage.

In our profession, due to the environment and the different personalities we have to deal with, we have to be careful not to gossip, put another stylist or barber down, or be judgmental about another's techniques or style. I learned that the enemy will use people to say negative things to mess up your spirit and get you to say negative things to hinder what God is doing in your life. Stylists will talk about the shop, the owner, and other stylists; and once the discord starts, they leave. Customers will get in your chair and gossip about other people, other stylists, their lifestyle, other people's sins, their jobs, and complain about life. Before you know it, you're talking and agreeing; but God showed me in His word that if two agree on anything, whether it's negative or positive, that word is being established in the earth. So be careful. I have learned that when other people say negative things and you believe something else, you will waiver. For example, a stylist or barber may say, "It's pretty slow today. All my customers are canceling." If you respond, "It sure is slow. I don't care if they come or not," you are speaking death to yourself. Instead, you may want to say, "God is my source, and I'm sure he will supply all my needs. My customers are on the way." God warned us in Matthew 12:37, by our words we are justified (shown right), and by our words we are condemned (shown wrong). Stylists and barbers, "life and death are in the power of the tongue and they that love shall eat the fruit thereof." (Prov. 18:21). So what have you been saying about your profession, your coworkers, your boss, your customers (when they aren't around), your pay, or your booth rentals? When no one is around, do you say, "I'm tired of this customer. They get on my nerves. They're so cheap. They never know what they want." If so, stop! Your problem is right in front of you. Your mouth could be the reason things are not happening for you in the workplace.

I have seen in my own business that when I say something negative about a customer or booth renter who is getting on my nerves, that customer or coworker eventually leaves, because I was speaking those things into existence. You must realize that some people can never see their faults, just yours. Love hides a multitude of faults. So don't let your mouth get you in trouble.

As a stylist, I ran into several problems with other stylists lying about me or telling me something another stylist said.

I would act like it didn't bother me. It was hard for me to believe that stylist was jealous of my clientele and how I work. However, God taught me that I had to start protecting my spirit, because what you hear can cause you to become bitter and have hidden hatred for that person. And it would cause you not to walk in the love of God that is put in your heart by the Holy Ghost. Proverbs 25:9 says, "Argue your case with your neighbor himself; discover not to disclose not a secret to another." Therefore, if you have a problem with another person (stylist, barber, owner, or customer), learn to talk to them and not discuss it with anyone else. I was often guilty of this, because when we are hurt, we sometimes want others to know how we feel.

Stylists, barbers, and owners, we have lost good customers, coworkers, and booth rentals because of our mouths. I encourage you to pray and ask the Holy Ghost to help you in this area, because it is a daily task. Proverbs 15:1 says that "a soft answer turns away wrath." So the next time a customer or coworker says something in anger, answer them softly. I was guilty of getting loud when someone got loud with me, until I learned that flesh begets flesh. Giving out anger gets anger. Giving out criticism receives criticism. I know what you are thinking at this point, because I have been asked many times, "Are you writing a book for the customers?" The answer is "No." When we get in order, the customers will follow suit. Remember, everything flows from the head (the owners and workers) to the body (the customers). There is so much I could write about on our mouths, but since the space I have does not permit it, I encourage you to meditate on these scriptures to help you with your mouth:

"A hypocrite with his mouth destroyeth his neighbor: but through knowledge shall the just be delivered." (Prov. 11:9)

"Every idle word that men speak they shall give account thereof, in the day of judgment, for by our words we are justified (shown right), by our words we are condemned (shown wrong)." (Matt. 12:36–37)

"The wicked is snared by the transgressions of his lips; but the just (uncompromisingly) shall come out of trouble." (Prov. 12:13)

"The words of a wise man's mouth are gracious, but the lips of a fool will swallow him up," (Ecc. 10:12). So many of us say we love God but we forget that God is love, and he said we will know his disciples by their love one for another. We are deceiving ourselves when we sit in our salons and talk about each other's with no regrets and talk about your clients before they can get out the salon. You need a heart- check when you are so jealous of your clients and other people's clients. Repent and get it right, so you can be blessed.

"If any man among you seems to be religious, and bridleth not his tongue, but deceiveth his own heart, this man's religion is vain (worthless)." (Jas. 1:26)

"Set a watch, O Lord, before my mouth; keep the door of my lips." (Ps. 141:3)

Let the words of my mouth and the meditation of my heart be acceptable in thy sight, oh Lord, my strength and my redeemer." (Ps. 19:14)

Remember texting is a form of communication so be careful because it can cause problems with clients, if you forget to respond, missed read the text or they put their feelings into your response. I didn't know text had feeling but I found out in this industry customers will put what they going through on you. I've learned if the conversation keeps going back and forth its best to call them. You must communicate with clients in your chair so you can please them, There is no way to build a cliental without talking to your clients, I didn't say gossip. You have to see what they like and don't like. I worked with a stylist that wouldn't say nothing to clients after she started on their head, she said that's my personality I said OK, but people going to think something is wrong with you and not want you over there crown. Stylist and barbers it also makes a workplace uncomfortable when you don't talk to your co-workers. After leaving my salon, the stylist no longer does hair. You must communicate and in Love.

Watch your words because your adversary the devil (his demons) are waiting to perform what you are saying. He that keeps his mouth keeps his life(business/ clients). Be quiet unless it helps someone, be Positive. I know we have to interact with our clients but if taking slows down your performance and causes you to move slower don't talk so much, clients want to go home. Plus you have other clients wishing you would speed up and stop all the talking. Use wisdom none of our clients are the same.

What changes could you make in this area that would help your life and business?

_____

_____

_____

_____

_____

_____

_____

_____

_____

_____

_____

_____

_____

_____

_____

_____

_____

_____

_____

_____

_____

_____

_____

_____

_____

_____

_____

_____

_____

2

Ten Commandments for Hairstylists

1. "Honor the Lord with thy substance and with the firstfruits of all thine increase (Prov. 3:9)
2. Report income and pay your taxes. God said, "Render therefore to all dues; tribute to whom tribute is due; custom to whom custom ; fear to whom fear; honour to whom honour (Rom. 13:7).
3. Be on time for appointments. If something changes, leave messages or try and contact your customers. Emergencies happen to all of us.
4. Ask God for the ability to be creative. Ask him how to increase your sales and how to manage your money. Attend classes to learn about investments in annuities, stocks, and bonds.
5. Support your business by purchasing the necessary tools, supplies, business cards, flyers, and equipment to get the job done. Stop being cheap and buy the things you need on a daily basis.
6. Pay your booth fee and vendors on time and stop avoiding your creditors. Treat them the way you want to be treated.

7. Don't be a respecter of person. Treat all customers the same, for "God is not a respecter of person" (Acts 10:34).
8. Don't gossip at all. Don't even discuss your personal business with your customers. Be led by the spirit of God. They will sometimes use it against you. Customers tend to want to gossip also; so be careful.
9. Be grateful to God for your work place and clients.
10. Keep a song in your heart, and keep your family before the Lord.

Ten Commandments for Barbers

1. "Honor God with the first fruit of all thine increase" (Prov. 3:9).
2. Report income and pay your taxes. God said "render unto Caesar what's due, and render unto God what's due" (Rom. 13:7).
3. Be on time for appointments and stop being a respecter of person. I have watched many barbers put friends, or people they feel are prestigious, ahead of other paying customers.
4. Stop gossiping and discussing other people when customers are in your chair. Refrain from ungodly chatter; it leads to more ungodliness. Remember, there are boys watching who look up to you. For some of them, you are the only father figure they see.

5. Pay your booth fee on time.

6. Expect to be appreciated. Continue to do well, and in due season, you will reap.

7. Don't get romantically involved with your clients, coworkers, or get involved with your customers' or coworkers' mate.

8. Support your business by purchasing the proper tool, supplies, and equipment to get the job done.

9. Be grateful to God and the owner who allows you to be part of their business.

10. Keep a song in your heart and keep your family before the Lord.

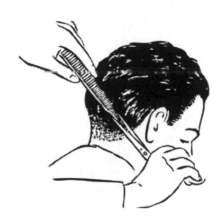

3

Seeds of Wisdom Regarding Our Clients

Professionals don't get upset when I discuss the issues that face us about our customers. I love my customers too; but in order for you to have the victory, I must tell the truth. Don't get me wrong, not all customers are a problem. I'm blessed to have great customers; but in order to help you run a successful business, we must deal with the minority. Old folks used to say, "One monkey can't stop no show," but since I've grown older, I've learned that one *can* stop a show, just like a bad apple can spoil the whole bunch if not taken out.

Stylists and barbers, I know I'm discussing a lot of things, but all these problems we're having are not the customers' fault. We create these problems by showing favoritism and spoiling certain customers. For example, we say to some, "Man, come on. I got you covered. You can pay me later" or "Girl, it's okay you're short. You can pay next week" or "Man, come on in. I'll write you down, nobody will know" or, "Girl, we went out last night. I owe you for those drinks" or "You did that for me with your business." Then when they take advantage of this, you get frustrated and take it out on everyone else. So stop what you have created. It's never too late. Talk to them, and let them know you messed up and now you have to get it right. You were only trying to help, and people took your kindness for granted.

Sometimes customers expect us to work miracles. They can be cruel, and no matter how we apologize, some of them will say, "I forgive you, but not enough to come back to you." It is important to realize we can't satisfy everyone. Customers have so many salons to choose from that they sometimes take us for granted. Oftentimes, customers come to us, aware they have hair problems. They come in for service a few times, but because they have not allowed us to properly perm or condition their hair, the problem still exists. They go out and deliberately try to ruin our name instead of truthfully stating what the previous stylist did to their hair, or what they themselves have been doing to their own hair to cause the problem.

When a customer comes to you with problem, I suggest you carefully explain all the possible results they could have from the treatment and care you provide. Have them sign an analysis sheet and a non-responsibility form. This is business, and we must also protect ourselves while providing the best, most honest service to our clients. I encourage this especially for those on medications. This is because, one time, I had a daughter and her mother came to me for hair care, and the mother was on dialysis two to three times a week. I took care of her hair to the best of my ability for about a year or so.

She had only thinning on her hairline. The mother asked me to use a press and comb in the jar, so that's what

I purchased. Then one day, they didn't show up or call. So I called the daughter at work and was told by her coworker that her mother's hair had fallen out and she was blaming me. She was saying I had used a strong perm on her mother's hair. This was the first time I had heard of her mother's problem. I cried till I couldn't cry anymore, and then I talked to God. I asked God to make a way for me to talk to the mother, which He did. I talked to her and told her I was sorry for what I had been accused of and that I used only a sensitive perm on her hair. She didn't seem to have any problems with me. I then went to God and asked him to have mercy on the daughter and to destroy every lie she had spoken about me. So be careful in this area.

When customers present pictures of styles they desire, we owe it to them to be honest if we don't think their hair texture or length will achieve the results they want. Advise the customers if extensions will be required to achieve the look. One big mistake we make is to send customers away unhappy when we know deep inside we wouldn't wear the particular style we gave them. The truth is, we really didn't know how to give them what they wanted. Realize that there are customers you may need to refer to another stylist or barber who specializes in a particular area. Doctors do this all the time.

When a customer requests bonding, inform them that the material in bonding glue is the same material used to make rubber tires, which can cause alopecia (hair loss). I'm guilty of putting a weave in a bald spot to satisfy a customer, and then realized I was only making matters worse. Be honest about any damage that a procedure may cause, even with sew ins. One sew in, quick weave, or braids can destroy a clients follicles especially if they already have issues. And trust me you will be the blame no matter how bad they wanted it.

Professionals if you have clients with medical condition or alopecia of any form please have them sign a no responsibility clause before rendering any service because trust me if they have any hair loss they will act like they didn't know or forgot all the warnings you gave them and come after your wallet. Clients will forget about your good name, your faithfulness towards them, all the prayers and make you out to be an insensitive monster, please take my word. Slow down and take the time to cover yourself and your establishment. Trust me if you don't it will come back to bite you in the butt.

Our customers sometimes share with us their fears, hurts, failures, successes, sicknesses, and details of family and personal relationships. If they trust us, we should pray for them and not discuss it with others. What we say is very important when listening to their problems, because we can speak life or death to any situation. Don't give your personal opinion, but tell them the truth with love and tell them what God's Word says, not your flesh.

Our clients hear our problems and know our lives as well. So be careful always putting your burdens and problems on them. They don't want to hear your mess all the time clients sometimes want to come in and get services and go home. It's not that they don't care they get tired like you of hearing there problems. If you keep discussing your unstable relationship and they gonna understand why you so unstable with them. When you get a mate you happy and don't come to work and treat them like nothing and when you need the money you expect them to be there, sorry it will catch up with you. So run a business and stop just doing hair. It hurt me to see how soon we forget how our clients have supported our business and stuck by us through our pain, sickness, and issues and soon as they go through we're so insensitive. You take them for granted by coming in late, overbooking, calling in, taking excessive breaks and being rude. I realize now that since most stylists and barbers have never worked a 9-5 job or in corporate America they have missed out on discipline and being accountable. I've heard them say I'm my own boss", I beg the differ, you have several bosses: the clients that's paying you for a service and they deserve respect. If you don't change your attitude it will show up in your bank account. The positive will be negative and you will struggle no matter how bad of a stylist /barber you are. You will walk around like you have it together but you know the truth. You will get mad at the supply person when they show up and question every charge even though you've been using there products for years. You will leave work early to avoid paying them and barely able to pay booth fee on time cause you will take the money you made early in the week to splurge with others and waste money instead of handling your first obligations. So please work on your attitude and you will see a difference.

We should speak life to our customers and believe God with them for their hair to be restored. Advise them to drink plenty of water, exercise, eat right, and take vitamins. God warned the people in Isaiah 3:24, it shall come to pass that instead of a well-set hair, they'd have baldness. Many of our customers lose their hair due to stress, sickness, improper diet, improper hair care, and unconfessed sin—to name a few causes. Thank God for His new covenant. Through it, our customers can have full hair restoration.

Accept constructive criticism so that your business can go to another level. Sisters and brothers, be advised that some people are intimidated by us having a lot of customers, so be careful. For some reason, people don't mind waiting for the doctor, dentist, mechanic, and grocery store clerk, but if we get off-schedule and run late, we hear complaints. Our revenue depends on the number of clients we see, so pray about this area and be careful how you book appointments. Don't allow walk-ins or call-ins to interrupt your scheduled customers. Get a backup tech or partner with another stylist when you are overbooked. Don't be afraid to tell customers what products or colors you are using, thinking that they will go somewhere else. They should know what is being used. Remove excess gel or color off the customer's skin, and drape customers properly to avoid sending them out of the salon wet.

Stylists and barbers are usually the last contact our customers have after a hard day's work, and we can get the bad end of the stick. Pray for them and work in as much love as possible. Be sympathetic, because some sisters and brothers are under tremendous stress mentally, financially, and physically. However, don't allow them to run over you. Keep your family in the forefront, because they go lacking when you're at the salon for long hours. Be careful not to discuss a customer with another customer, especially when a problem has occurred. I was guilty of this at times, and it is wrong. You may think it's harmless but the enemy will use it against you, and you will lose clients. Be careful. Customers will hurt your business out of jealousy or their own inner motives. Show your customers you appreciate them by offering discounts on particular days. Send them a thank-you, birthday, or anniversary card. I also advise stylists to retail products to their customers, so that between visits, they're using the same products you use on their hair.

Stop crying over customers that have left you regardless of why they left. Pray about it and move on. Stop looking back at your old appointment book. The enemy would sometimes lead me to call up old customers and apologize when I knew I hadn't done anything wrong! I would even beat myself up over it!

In one month, I had seven regular, good-paying customers leave me. Some of them didn't even tell me, and they had been around for years. However, the Holy Spirit revealed it to me. In prayer, God spoke softly to me, "When I start pruning (cutting off), don't complain. I know what's best for you." Everything has a season, so don't cry when a customer's season is over with you. It's not to hurt you but to sometimes take you to another level in your business. Paul warned us to put those things behind us and press forward to a higher calling in Christ Jesus (Phil. 3:13–14).

Please don't cut a customer hair unless they want it or you've explain why they need it and the extra cost. Because clients tend to try and not pay for there hair cuts, its artistry so get paid for it. When you say "end clip," clip the ends. So many customers are discouraged with salons due to bad haircuts. Be honest. If you don't know how to cut a particular style, refer them to someone else. Take haircutting classes and attend hair shows to advance in this area. Use protective creams on customers when applying any chemical. It is unfair to the customer for you to protect yourself and not them.

Let clients know in advance if children are not welcome. Don't wait until they show up to show your dismay. Just express in love that you prefer for them not to bring their children, because it's important for all customers to be able to relax. It's hard for them to watch their kids and receive services at the same time. I have had customers' kids tear up stylist's books, break items, mess up the shop, and as soon as I said something to the parent, they got upset. Be consistent with all clients, it's not fair to your co-workers or other clients to see a particular client be allowed to bring their child regularly and nor receiving Services. Don't make excuses for your clients, by saying "I don't' know why they don't want kids here" knowing they get on your nerves as well. Clients don't take their kids when they go out with the girls, boys, doctor appointment or where ever they go for their personal time. Plus it can be a liability on the salon if the child falls, gets hurt or pick up a hot element. It's best to deal with this up front.

Stylists and barbers, please be careful when doing other stylists' customers—even if you all agree to it. The enemy (the devil) will sometimes use customers to play us against one another over price differences. Discuss your prices because you may not charge the same, and they can't expect you to. The customers will even compare your styling technique. Be sensitive to your coworker's feelings. It's important that you stress to your customers to make appointments, because you will be taking days off sometimes to spend time with family. Doing this will help keep them from walking in and expecting services, only to get upset when they see that you're off work. Let's keep it real, some customers are going to get offended because they just don't like setting appointments or being on time.

Stylist and barbers when walk-in come to the salon don't overcharge them because you see extra money. I've seen so many of you do this for the money or because you have a certain goal they were trying to reach and the client never returns to the salon. I've seen others add ten or fifteen dollars extra and the style didn't even look great. You should continue building a clientele and remember when you do this to people, you will reap it back somewhere in your business dealings or when you are receiving services somewhere There's nothing like a client getting in your chair, you servicing them, and they then ask if they can pay you later. This has happened to the best of stylist and barbers in the industry. All I can tell you is keep your tone right, and if you have to do it one time, explain to the client that you won't be able to do it again. For some reason they love to count our money and feel we can wait. They don't do it at stores they like to shop at. They pay with some form of money. They don't consider you have a supply bill, booth rental, insurance and estimated taxes and other bills to pay. I have seen so many client relationships damaged from extending credit. I avoid it altogether. You do what's best for you. I can only tell you by the wisdom of God what works best. I love my clients, but I've always had the attitude that I am running a business. Guess what? When I did try and work with a lady on fixed income the day I responded back to her text and told her I couldn't , she got offended .sent me ugly text and never came back. Yes it hurts when you've only been good to them but you will get over it and God will send you other clients. So don't create no monsters that you will have to kill later. It's nothing personal, men and women.

Also, when you get a new customer, please don't allow them to talk negatively about their previous stylist to you. I found that most of the time they are coming to you for a reason, perhaps because they are mad at their stylist for whatever reason. Once that customer gets over their anger, they'll leave without saying goodbye, telling their stylist they missed them, and never apologizing for the negative things they said to others.

Stylists and barbers, you must be very careful not to hurt other stylists or to allow customers to play games and start confusion in your salon. Some sisters and brothers will see another person's work and go to the other person without saying anything, just to cause a problem. I had customers whose eyebrows I arched, and when they decided to go to another stylist, they would come in and not even speak to me. Ask yourself why. There are salons everywhere. Some customers will wait until they know you are off to see someone else in the salon instead of going elsewhere. Always consult God. He doesn't want us building on another man's foundation. You reap what you sow. It's a trick of the devil to get people in strife and to hurt your feelings. Also, I learned that people who profess to be Christians are sometimes the hardest customers to deal with. I would get offended because of small things the customer would do. For example, some customers have complained that their hairdo didn't last when they knew that it had rained or their shower had been too hot or they had engaged in extra-curricular activities. I had to learn that instead of getting upset, I had to tell the truth in love, walk in love, and work on better self-control.

Let customers know if they bring in their own preferred products whether your pricing will change, so any problems or misunderstandings can be avoided. Respect your customer's time, shop and pay bills on your time. Don't leave the customers unattended; especially when you know that what you're doing will take longer than expected. Stylists and barbers, take scheduled breaks to take care of your personal business. To leave a client at salon while you go shopping, to a funeral or on a date is horrible. Stylist and barbers have the nerves to say the industry is changing. No you are selfish and feel because you are self-employed you can do anything. I advise you to get it together.

Post prices or make brochures of your services, so your customers know what you charge. I've had customers hand me their usual fee, knowing they received extra services. Let customers know if you allow credit. I've had customers wait until I was finished to write me a postdated check, without discussing it with me first before coming for their appointment. We must insist that everything be done decently in order to avoid confusion. Just because a customer comes regularly doesn't mean you have to give them a discount all the time. I shop at some stores all the time, and I don't expect a discount. If it's on sale, I'm grateful to God. The store clerks always make sure they say, "Thanks, come again." Realize that you are running a business.

In Jeremiah 22:13, God said to the kings, "Woe unto him that buildeth his house by unrighteousness, and his chambers by wrong; that useth his neighbor's service without wages, and giveth not for his work." In other words, we are paid for services we render. If another stylist helps you, pay her. It's wrong to make money and not pay your co-worker, doesn't matter if she/he is your friend. Especially when they are trying to make it in the industry and you have a large clientele. Their backs and legs get tired as well. be afraid to charge for the services you render either. If you decide to give your customer a complimentary service, make sure you let them know the regular cost. Customers will talk to other customers and make them feel like you are charging them and not everyone. For some strange reason, customers get upset when you bless them with a partial perm or cut then charge them another time, so I've learned to have them pay; but be led by the spirit of God on this issue.

Stylists and barbers, please avoid credit! Many problems can result from extending credit; the worst of which is being forced out of business, as well as the loss of good friendships. Over the years, I've had customers angry at me about a *bad* check they wrote to me! A good way to avoid the potentially costly trap of covering bad check charges is to post a return check fee in the salon or purchase a check/ Visa terminal to process all transactions. If you have to run to the bank every time you receive a check to make sure you receive your funds, I encourage you not to accept them. That's unnecessary travel and stress.

Don't be a respecter of persons. God sees everything. Use good products on all your customers, not just your favorites—especially if they're paying for that same service. Let customers know how important their scheduled appointment is. If they are going to be more than thirty minutes late, they may have to wait or reschedule, because they will be going into your next scheduled appointment. I encourage you to pray a lot about your scheduling.

I once had a customer who came for services with her two daughters every two weeks. Their days changed regularly due to school activities, and I worked with them, even if that meant staying later than normal. Then one day, the mother told me as she was leaving that she would most likely see me in two weeks on a Thursday. I wrote it down and planned to see them then unless she called and said differently. When that week came, she called on Wednesday and asked if I was expecting them. I told her that I was not. I was expecting them on Thursday. She then told me about two special things the girls had to be in on Thursday and Friday. After hanging up—even though I had other plans—I thought about it, cancelled my date, and called her back. She indicated she had been offended earlier and I apologized, even when I knew I hadn't done anything wrong. She said they were coming but then called back and said they weren't. It hurt me because I felt that as long as I had been willing to accommodate them, they were willing to accept it; but at the first sign of a problem, they became offended. I learned a valuable lesson in this—that is, to trust God. That customer never returned, and four other clients she had referred never came back either. Customers will leave you then plant seeds (negative words) in the earth to produce a harvest that affects your business. But Guess what? Yu can't curse what God has Blessed. I was blessed with a family of four that didn't want or need a family discount, required less work. tipped me and gave me something every holiday. I've been blessed to have them for

15 years now. God is awesome. The devil meant it for evil but God worked it out for my good cause I'm called for his purpose.

Stylist and barbers, make sure to ask a client what service they are getting done; there's nothing more frustrating to have a regular client come in and add a service that takes almost thirty minutes to an hour to perform, which throws your whole schedule off. It will cause your attitude to shift if you're not sensitive to the spirit of God and your day to shift. So tread lightly because the client won't care what you have on the books; they want what they want. I've learned to be kind and let them know if I'm unable to do it. I've seen where a client who never wants color, weave, or pin-up wants something different, and as a professional, you offered it at some point, and they aid "No, I don't like that." But if they get in a relationship or have a special event, that will change. That's fine; just ask client first so you can operate properly.

Also be careful if you offer to help a client by purchasing their extensions for them, especially if it's their first sew in. Because if they don't like it for whatever reason, you will be blamed and expected to compensate them in some way. It's an easy way to lose a client and sometimes not even know it just trying to be helpful. Have clients sign Hair extensions non-responsibility form to cover yourself.

Also don't let clients dictate to you what services you offer. If you don't do natural hair, don't do it. Refer them to a natural hair specialist. Sometimes they don't want to pay their prices, and soon as you do something they don't like, you could possibly be put on social media in a negative way or talked about to others.

People are sometimes led by their flesh, not the spirit of God. But if I'm providing excellent service, why would I allow another person to dictate my life? I know that sometimes we are so attached to people we don't tell them when they are wrong.

Stylists and barbers, I know I said a lot in regards to our customers, but you have to accept the truth in situations. God has blessed me with awesome clients, but I still have challenges. I try to show them I appreciate them in regards to their birthdates, anniversary, their time, and during holidays. I'm grateful for those who, when my season of doing their hair was over, we remained friends. Please accept the fact that customers have a right to spend their money wherever they choose, as long as it doesn't cause conflict in your work place.

Here are three ways to know a season is almost over with a client. God doesn't want us to be overwhelmed, but have peace in all we do. So, be encouraged and know God will provide what you need.

1. They start complaining of small things and compare your work to others.
2. The client will accuse you of something. For example, breakage, not giving them the style they want, or not agreeing with your price increase.
3. They make an appointment and are a no-call, no- show.

Stylists and barbers, if you confess to be Christian, I encourage you not to just build your clientele on church folks. I've learned that people who haven't accepted Christ sometimes treat you better than the so-called born-again

Christian. Use the time in your chair to be a light to the unsaved person. "Let your light shine before men that they may see your good works, and glorify your Father which is in heaven," (Matt. 5:16). How do we do that? We let our light shine by showing them the love of God.

At one time, I was doing hair for several of my church members. One day, God spoke to me and told me to leave a denomination and go to a church that believed in the full council of God, not just what they wanted to do. I still loved God, but customers from my previous church left me one by one because I wasn't at that same building with them, even though I was still a member of the body of Christ. It hurt at first, but I asked God, "Why did they leave me when I'm your child, trying to live according to the Word?" He showed me in the Word that it's because they have a form of godliness but deny the power thereof (2 Tim. 3:5), Yes they go to church faithfully, sing in the choir, teach classes, but don't honor God's Word. Ephesians 5:11 says, "Take no part in and have no fellowship with the fruitless deeds and enterprises of darkness, but instead let our lives be so in contrast as to expose and reprove and convict them." Now I must be honest. God wanted me to be sensitive when talking to others about Him. You don't want to hurt people, and you have to accept that some of us won't go farther due to tradition and our leaders.

I began to pray more for the clients' hairs I worked on. This is serious, because you are dealing with all types of human spirits and personalities. Here I was having an awesome day, and then a client would come in with an ugly spirit. That spirit would affect the atmosphere of the salon, even my spirit. It took me a while to understand this, so I began to pray that the blood of Jesus cover my mind, body, and soul on a consistent basis, because I didn't want to pick up any unclean spirits or negative influences that would change the atmosphere of my salon. I asked God to give me strength to endure and know the season with my clients. In Ecclesiastes 3:1, Solomon warned us that "to everything there is a season, and a time for every matter and purpose under heaven."

I asked God to give me strength to deal with clients, who are talking bad about me or my service but smiling in my face, not taking responsibility for the things they would do to their hair or their daughter's hair and would try to blame me. God said, "Just walk in love." The Holy Spirit spoke to me and said, "Stop trying to hold onto this season (certain customers). It's over." I replied, "But it's the people I've loved that hurt me." God said, "That's okay. Change is good, and that client may need to be seen by a new pair of eyes."

Then I found where David said in Psalm 55:12–14:

> For it was not an enemy that reproached me; then I could have borne it: neither was it he that hated me that did magnify himself against me; then I would have hid myself from him: But it was thou, a man mine equal, my guide, and mine acquaintance, We took sweet counsel together, and walked unto the house of God in company."

Let people talk and say untruths, because God is the

judge. He warns us in Obadiah 1:15: "The day of the Lord is near upon all the heathen: as thou hast done, it shall be done unto thee: thy reward shall return unto thine own head."

I share this, because dealing with clients and their different personalities can be a challenge. I remember one client who would always come in and question how many clients I had done. I prayed for this jealous spirit, and within a month, she left. Glory to God, because he warns us that "jealousy is cruel as the grave," (Song of Sol. 8:6).

Stylists and barbers, if you want to do something special for clients, do it at the workplace or somewhere special, not at your home. Also, don't talk too much about the things you have purchased, because for some strange reason, people don't mind for their doctors, lawyers, politicians, or teachers to prosper; but when it comes to us, it's a problem. I have even heard people say, "If it wasn't for me going faithfully, he or she wouldn't have that," as if they are not receiving a service. I'm not saying not to be excited about the blessings of God, just use wisdom and know when to talk. Everybody's not happy for you.

Know when to stop taking clients. Your body and mind get tired and frustrated. I realized it's not good to accept clients who are hard to please at the end of the day. Tension will cause you to become frustrated, respond incorrectly, and not go the extra mile—especially if it's a customer that nitpicks all the time. Yes, the customers deserve to get what they are paying for, but not at the expense of causing you more pain. When clients always nitpick and criticize you or your technique, I encourage you to release them, because before it's over, he or she will find a major reason to leave you. So avoid the pain. I found out it's normally the client with hair problem who doesn't want to accept it, and nothing is good enough to them. I use the example, because hair is a living organism that has to be taken care of, just like a relationship. You can't start out one way then start doing different things and expect good results. Hair will die, like anything else that is not nourished. You can tell clients a fabric, necklace, or collar at the nape line can cause breakage and they will ignore it, until the damage is totally done. Then comes the blame game.

Warn clients about too much gel, spritz, or moisturizers, which they continue to use. When damaging results occur, I encourage you to keep your spirit up and do the best you can. I encourage you—regardless of the new styles(lace fronts, wigs, braids)—to always stick to the basics, because hair loss in women—especially, African American women— will take real hair care to restore. Every woman wants to be able to look at their hair at one point or another, though they may never admit it. Also tell your clients about the products you're using and retail them for in between visits, so they won't waste money and ruin their hair with different products on the market that aren't effective at all.

Stylists, we have to be honest with ourselves. So many people say we are over processing their hair, causing it to thin, and yes, some of us are. Go back to the basic of applying relaxer. If you are relaxing the whole head or half the head on each week or every 2 weeks, the hair can do nothing but break off and thin out. Customers are saying some of us want to make money so bad, we perm, perm, and perm. If you have to retouch every three to four weeks, you need to check the customer's texture and the relaxer system you're using. I know we all have different textures and growth patterns. You can't use a super or a no-lye on all clients. Stop being cheap and invest in the different types to be successful (mild, sensitive, regular, super), because if you continue to break and thin customers' follicles, the word will get out.

If you have neglected to care for your clientele's hair, dust yourself off and correct the problem. Be honest and start using good conditioning systems. Let your client know that deep conditioners are extra and they won't mind paying, because there's nothing like a healthy head of hair. I promise that investment in a good conditioning system will be profitable to you and the client. We should stop being in a hurry, condition the hair, and recommend regular haircuts.

Stylists and barbers, please don't make the same mistakes I made. When customers or coworkers lie about you, don't worry and try and defend yourself, especially when you know your heart is pure and you did your best. God warned us in Prov. 12:19 that "the lip of the truth shall be established and that a lying tongue is only for a moment." Stylists and barbers don't get upset. I want to help you. If you have children, please don't turn the salon into a day care. People will not be honest with you, but they don't want to be bothered with you dealing with your kids while they are paying you for a service. Before telling you, they will find another stylist to take care of their hair care needs. I know there may be times when you have to bring your children, but remember, this is your job. Your coworkers may not want to be bothered either, when trying to service clients as well.

I encourage some stylists and barbers to really seek God to

make sure this is your calling. I know you may enjoy hair, but God is a God of increase. God doesn't want you struggling to pay booth fees, buy supplies, and barely make it. Luke 13:6 tells of a man planting a fig tree that God had sought fruit of for three years, and it was not productive. The Lord told him to cut it down because of its unproductivity. The man asked for one more year to nurture it to see if it would bear fruit well; if not, it would be cut down. God didn't want the tree taking up space where something else could be growing. In other words, in our profession, God doesn't want you just wasting time, not being productive, or taking up space. If you have the same customers after three years, I encourage you to go to classes, mentor with others, and ask people close to you what you are doing wrong, because the truth will set you free. If things don't change, I encourage you to pray and ask God to show you your true calling. This may be a hard pill to swallow, but pride goes before destruction and a haughty spirit before a fall (Proverbs 16:18).

Also, stylists and barbers, stay encouraged when customers or others say negative things about your profession. I've heard some say, "I can cut my own hair," "People are tired of wasting time in these shops," "I can save that money, it's not worth it," "I can go to the neighborhood barber/stylist," "I can do my hair better than them," or "I'm going natural" to name a few. That's okay. Stay encouraged. Trust God, because there are clients all over the world that trust God, and no matter the situation, they are able to go to the salon every week or two. I read that in the Great Depression, people got their hair done to keep their spirits up and to feel better. Hallelujah.

Male hairstylists, be very careful when servicing women

clients because women sometime have an ulterior motive, and the enemy will send them purposefully to destroy your business or relationship. Some see you as a free-hair fix and you may see them as a booty call. Be wise, men.

Stylist and barbers, please don't loan money or do things for your clients. For example decorate a party, make clothes for them, help them move or whatever you do on the side, even though most of us are multitalented. This is the quickest way to lose a client, because as soon as they can't pay you, they will stop coming to the salon, or worse, some will lie like you are a bad stylist/barber knowing he or she owes you. Release them from the debt, and God will deal with them. If this happens to you and you know you owe someone repent and make it right. Things happen to us in this way sometimes because we've done it to others. Some of us claim to be so professional but don't see how rude it is to be talking on a Bluetooth to your family and friends while servicing them. Yes, you are self-employed, but you're at work, and they are paying you. Then soon as your clients stop coming, you say it's the enemy. You never take the time to see how long you have your clients waiting just to get styled out.

Also, you need to ask God for a heart-change when you can service a client and you are talking about them before he/she can leave the salon or your co-workers clients before they come in or leave. Remember other clients are listening and may not return feeling like you will do them the same. Don't be used by the devil to run your co-workers clients off. You have serious issues to deal with, because I promise you, other clients are listening, and you will destroy your own business. Some other stylist and barber's clients will leave for that reason because they don't like the atmosphere. Be careful when discussing everyday life issues, politics, ideas, children, lifestyles in the salon because clients listen as they get involved, but you never will know if something you said may have offended them because of their views, religion, or past hurt.

Also remember that is only your client while they are I your chair, they can choose to go where ever they like and spend their money where ever they choose. So thank God when you have faithful clients. Professionals if you choose to work 2 jobs to supplement your income that's your choice. Don't make the customers suffer by coming in tired, complaining, rushing and half doing their hair. Some clients just stay with you because they love you, so be grateful. One day they will get tired of paying you and see other people hair that looks awesome and leave you. So get rest and schedule them when you will be able to perform 100 percent.

I pray the examples I've given you will be a blessing to you and your business, and that you will learn from my mistakes. So I encourage you to pray, pray, pray. "Pray without ceasing. In everything give thanks. For this is the will of God in Christ Jesus for you," (1 Thess. 5:17–18).

Stylist and barbers you make a huge mistake putting a family member or non-regular client on your regular clients appointment time and have them waiting for hours. Clients are watching and they will make comments to let you know because they don't appreciate it. Also professionals you need a heart check when you are always combative(argumentative) with your clients, you never heard the saying "don't bite the hand that feed you". Abuse people have a tendency to abuse others. So ask God for deliverance.

If you have a client that loves attention, can be loud and obnoxious I advised you to deal with it early because one day it will get out of hand. Deal with you client and let he/she no it's not acceptable behavior in your workplace. Don't let them discuss sex or use profanity in the salon.

If you see a client sleep under the dryer and their head not properly drying be kind enough to let the stylist know so she can adjust the dryer or the client so they can still get out in a timely manner, I've seen stylist laugh and not say nothing. We have to all work together to have great customer service. And don't leave client under dryer for hours to finish up on another client, at least take them out and let them wait. I've seen stylist see the client sweating or having hot flashes and don't do nothing. At least offer the client some water.

Also, if you as a stylist/barber have clients that love to swap chairs in the salon and says "I can spend my money with whoever and whenever I want" that may be true, but not in your establishment especially if the customer is messy and just trying to create problems. Watch that spirit, because it sneaky and will plant seeds of discord in the salon.

Please don't allow no customer to come in talk about your co-workers in any way. If you do, get a heart check because it's something in you that wants to hear it. We work so many hours in the salon that it's more like a family, Oh I forgot most families do talk about each and have issues, but that don't make it right.

I had to get in my word and keep my heart right because even being a Christian we are human. Yes, I would get angry when a client calls and cancel at last minute and have me getting up early, or call me several times for an appointment and then cancel, or tell me something another client said. I would not curse them out, but roll my eyes or let them know I didn't appreciate it and next time don't call me unless they are sure, or text them with the wrong response and cause an offense. The bible says "be angry but sin not: let not the sun go down upon your wrath. Neither give place to the devil Eph. 4: 26-27 In other words, don't go to bed mad because you may not wake up to make it right. And when you open the door to the devil he will use it to destroy your clientele or business. I'm a living witness, so I'm only trying to help you not make the same mistakes. So I made a choice to run my business and not let my business run me, walk in love, say things with a better tone. use self-control, keep a positive attitude and know that God is with me. I had to keep my heart right so my facial expressions would be right cause what's on the inside will show on the outside. Stop making excuses for your looks towards other and get it right. Be consistent with all clients and do your work as unto the Lord (Colossians 3:23) and you and your clients will be great. I'm blessed to have clients for over 15 years and they love me and I Love them. I encourage you to ask God for wisdom in all situations.

Professional don't allow clients to control the thermostat in your workplace. We have to be considerate that our coworkers are working and clients should be comfortable as well. Clients go everywhere)doctor, dentist, hospital) and it's cold and don't complain, they dress cordially and they should respect our salons and do the same. Stylist and barbers you should dress properly to your body, just because it's winter don't mean we don't have to turn the air on. If you stay hot dress loosely. I've learned it's not the air that gives us the colds it's the germs we not killing with the air. Clients shouldn't be allowed to pick dryers or control the television, stop allowing clients to run you and run a professional business.

Prayer / Confessions about Your Customers

Heavenly Father, bless my customers to be satisfied with the services I render. If they're not, bless them and have them tell me with love, so I can rectify any problems. Bless my customer's finances so they can consistently receive good hair care.

I declare that you are Jehovah Jireh, and you will provide my customers with the necessary finances to purchase products to care for their hair between appointments. I declare that my customers will be on time for appointments; they will call and cancel in a timely manner. They will walk in agape love (the God kind of love) toward me, my family, and friends. I declare that my customers will pay me properly. Bless my clients to have a good attitude towards me, my co-worker and salon owner. Let them speak only words that build up and edify and if not let conviction come so they can make the necessary changes.

In Jesus's Holy name. Amen.

4

Seeds of Wisdom for Salon Owners

This may be a touchy subject, because there are some great salon owners and some extremely bad owners. Instead of talking about them, let's start praying for them; because where you work represents you also. I've seen many stylists/barbers get jealous and start complaining about everything when God gives an owner more stylists. We must start being excited when our salon owners prosper. I've been guilty of complaining at times during my career, and it profits nothing!

I've worked at three salons in my career. At two of them, I left by force, not by choice. The first shop closed and turned into a day care center with one week's notice. The other was vandalized. All my equipment were stolen, and the owner did nothing to rectify the problem. The 3rd salon I managed for 9 years and my season just came to an end. As of this writing, I now operate my own salon.

I try to be a great owner but I have to check myself out as well. I don't mind getting things done but sometimes with life problems I would tell the stylist to come to me but I realized I wasn't always receptive or respond properly or keep my facials right. I would listen and get it done but my spirit wasn't right, I had to remember they're not thinking about your issues or the stress I had been under losing a brother, husband getting sick and just the day to day operation, they just want things done because it's the right thing to do with their clients coming and paying their money to work there. I make no excuses I just had to admit it and work on myself. And yes some workers just nick pick and that can be frustrating. but the Lord told me to not focus on the ones always complaining if it's time for them to leave they will in due time. You can't sweat the small stuff they want something different or they out grow where they are that's fine, we all like and need change, just stay positive.

A wise salon owner told me don't be calling all those meeting for a complainer that expects everything to be perfect. God is the only perfect one but, we can have a spirit of excellence. They will have you have the meeting and you going to run everyone else off because they are going to know who doing all the complaining against them. The best thing to do is be a good leader and go to the stylist individually about what they are doing and ask them to correct it, especially when it's affecting the workplace and others. They may not care if it affects there clientele but most of the time it does and they don't get it until it's too late. Proverbs12:1 says whoever loves discipline loves knowledge, but he who hates correction is stupid. Don't get mad at me that what the bible says and I've learned it to be true. Also be careful of the worker that always demand a lot and have you spending, spending they will be the first one to leave.

Many owners neglect their responsibilities, mainly because some of them don't work as stylists. Owners, please invest in your salon by painting, replacing fixtures, and fixing water leaks, to name a few. Clients are tired of paying good money to come into an unkempt salon, and booth renters are tired of having to ask you to repair things. Little things go undone, such as not keeping soap and tissue in restrooms, not repairing hair dryers, not stocking snack machines, and poor shop maintenance, in general. Remember, it's "the small foxes that spoil the vine" (Song of Sol. 2:15).

Booth renters get fed up with shops that are not maintained, and many leave without notice and with unpaid debts. Of course, this isn't right either. If you are guilty of leaving someone's salon, I urge you to call them, apologize, repent, put your pride aside, and settle your debts. Remember, you reap what you sow, you may be a salon owner one day and it will all return to you.

Salon and barber shop owners, we need to reevaluate how we look at booth renters, because without them, you won't be successful. Owners stop coming in because you had a bad night changing the television or radio when others are watching or listening to it. That's so rude. Handle that in a better way. Stop making a scene in front of the clients for things that are out of order, unless it's something that will get you shut down immediately. I had to learn to trust them to deal with their own clients and if the issue continues then I say something. Clients receive better from there stylist, just don't throw the owner under the bus by saying "The owner said" as if you don't agree. Remember you reap what you sow and they will be saying to themselves you are so phony and please you really will be called a phony Christian if you confess to be one.

Professionals, treat another person's salon as if it were yours. We can't allow our customers or their children to tear up the place. Our customers drop trash and leave food and cans around; some of us walk right by it. It's not right. You may need a heart-check if you feel you're too good to empty the trash, especially when your customers eat in the shop. The Word says in Ecclesiastes 9:10, "Whatever your hands find to do, do it with thy might for in the grave where you are going, there is neither working, or planting, nor wisdom."

Stylists and barbers don't get mad. It's our responsibility as booth renters to take our trash out and keep our areas in accordance to the State Board regulations; especially if you allow your clients to eat in your area. Regardless of the situation, show your owner you appreciate him or her by simply turning off appliances, helping to keep the salon clean, answering the telephone, answering the door, or reporting when something is wrong. Be considerate and don't turn a dryer on fifteen to twenty minutes early; it only takes two to four minutes for dryers to get hot. Don't talk about your salon owner to your clients. You are only destroying your own clientele and cause them to dislike the owner, which leads them not to come and get services from you. Don't think I am trying to justify these shop owners that hold meetings and never do what they say or never show appreciation for you, even though you're self- employed. I'm just telling you what's best for you, to grow, and allow God to work on them. Have you ever thought that your owner needs to be encouraged or just told the truth so they can look at things in another way and make the necessary changes?

Pray for your boss, who talks in between stylists, causing confusion? God knows everything. If your season is up at a salon, don't leave in anger, leave in peace—like the Word of God says. Also, please stop trying to go into another's business and change things, especially the atmosphere. Before you accept employment in a salon, ask the owner for references, talk to the other stylists and customers, and see if you really want to work there. If, after working there, it's not what you desire, then leave and don't go putting out negative words on the salon afterwards. When God tells you to leave, no matter what the problems are, make sure you leave, because the spirit of God told you to and not your flesh. "For you shall go out with joy, and be led forth with peace," (Isa 55:12). If you go into a salon that plays jazz music and you like rap music, don't start playing rap music and being loud. Find a salon that fits your personality. I have seen many stylists start discord in salons over things they didn't like. Please, if you agree to work in a salon and agree to the guidelines set by management; don't play your clients against the owner or manager. It's your responsibility to deal with your clients, who are loud, disrespectful, cursing, bringing kids, or eating all over the shop. Don't say, "The manager said...". Tell them or call the client to correct the problem. If you don't want to confront the small issues, you need to find a salon conducive to what you want to accept. Trust me, if you don't deal with it, the problem will get bigger. Plus, it's wrong to make your manager or owner look like a bad person.

You should have peace wherever you go. Something is wrong if you drag yourself every day to the salon, because your spirit isn't at peace. Take it from me, get out. We, especially Christians, shouldn't have to cover our spirit every time we step in the door with other believers who are our coworkers. Trust God if you have to relocate. About those customers that act like they're with you and don't come with you, trust me, God will give you new clients. When I moved, some of my clients didn't come, and some complain of the extra ten-minute drive, but God still took care of me. I managed a beauty shop for eight years and was never appreciated. It wasn't the manager's fault, it was mine. I have learned in the Word of God that we should be treated well, and I should have loved myself more than to be used by others. I have learned not to give my pearls to the swine, they will trample over it. In others words, stop planting in bad soil and expect to reap a good harvest. Get excited because every seed you plant leaves your hand but never leaves your life. It will produce a harvest somewhere in your life. Don't expect it from the people you are good to, God has a way of getting the harvest to you!

Stylists and barbers, if one of your coworkers should move to another salon, support them by telling customers where they are and give the number if you have it. It's wrong to try and hinder someone else's business, because your heart is not right. I warn you not to try and build on another man's foundation. I remember when I relocated, and the owner took my number off the voice mail three days later, knowing some clients usually come by every six to eight weeks. Yes, it hurt, but the Holy Spirit reminded me that no weapon that is formed against me would prosper (Isa. 54:17). God blessed my clients to find me.

Salon owners, God is going to hold you accountable when you bring in new stylists and do not keep your promises to help them. Instead you as well as other stylist grab all the walk-ins and referrals, knowing that the new stylists need to build his/her clientele. These types of behavior hurt the new stylist or barber and cause them to become discouraged with the industry. If it's a service he/ she can't perform, that's understandable, because you want the client to be satisfied and to come again.

Stylists and barbers, I can't believe so many of us want to manage a salon or go solo but can't submit to someone at the shop where you're at. Just because you have a nice clientele doesn't mean you have to open up a salon. Management and communication skills are very important. When everyone is a problem, maybe you need to look in the mirror. God said, "where there is unity, he commands a blessing," (Ps. 33:1–3). Remember that whatever you give out will come back "pressed down running over men will give unto your bosom" (Lk. 6:38).

Salon owners, I know I've encouraged the stylist and barbers to do what is right, but you also must do right by them, whether you are in the salon or not. You're making money, whether they are on commission or booth rental, and it's okay to live off the money you make, but it's wrong to never invest in the salons upkeep. Some of you inform stylists that clean towels are included in their booth fee, then they come to work and have none to service the clients. You tell them not to eat at work station but never try to provide a breakroom area. It's your responsibility to keep soap, tissue, and cleaning supplies in your establishment. Why set rules for your salon and not abide by them yourself? Some of you allow your family and friends to come in and do whatever they want to, and you wonder why the stylists leave, and then you have the audacity to talk about them forgetting when you haven't been a good steward over what God has given you. You tell them no gossiping or talking about coworkers, but you're the ring leader who is causing confusion in your establishment. Be careful in getting romantically involved with your coworkers. It can destroy a shop, especially when you run in to financial problems and the person you let get away with everything, doesn't pay. Then you take it out on the entire staff.

Beware of those stylists who are previous salon owners to come to work in your salon, because their motives aren't always pure. You will think they have been in your position and they will be great to have, but that's not always the case. Sometimes, they will be the biggest complainers to affect your salon out of their jealous heart, especially when their salon fails. I see why some stylist and barbers work alone, they never want to see themselves and when they get with others, they are afraid of what they can't do. As long as there is no comparison for them or the client, they are okay; but as soon as they see something better— especially the service—they will run again or get new ideas and leave. Hold your head up, you will get other stylist. Be aware of older stylist/barbers since they tend to keep messing up, because they are not used to how things work. They will leave your salon and try to get others to leave. I've heard them tell clients they unavailable and can't come in, then say business is slow here, instead of just leaving with a good attitude.

Stylist and barbers will talk amongst each other and say they self-employed when you need a shop meeting or you don't know their schedule but they want you to give them free booth rental or pay them for lost of income when they are leasing the space whether they are in or not. I can understand that too, but the bills still have to be paid. When you lease a house or apartment you can leave all you want and not be there but they expect there money. So do what can for them, but don't feel bad if you not in the position to do it. I've seen stylist make $ 1000 a week and barely want to give you the booth fee and wait to the last minute, its sad but its true. Keep a pure heart and trust me it will be ok.

Salon owners, trust me, most stylists/barbers don't want to leave their workplace and displace their clients, but you can't keep expecting them to accept anything—just like you shouldn't. When you have someone leave just evaluate what you could have done different but don't beat up on yourself. Correct the negative and stay positive. Remember the same Way clients have a seasons so does the staff. I encourage you to pray and get your heart right as well and ask God for the wisdom and resources to do what you need to do to keep your salon running successful. And then you will have a great styling team. Not everybody wants to run a salon, they love booth rental and going home. I know because I enjoyed having no responsibility other than to keep my area in order, help out where I was needed, and to be a blessing to the owner. Now I'm reaping the harvest, with great coworkers that pick up donuts, empty the trash, check the bathrooms, answer the phones, and treat my salon like it's their home. I appreciate all of them so much and I try to show them not just in words but in deeds.

Prayer for Salon Owners

Heavenly Father, in the name of Jesus, _____ bless to be a good owner. Bring _____ into the knowledge of Christ that he/she will get wisdom and knowledge to prosper in his/her business. Bless _____ to have the finances to maintain his/her salon, because it represents me also. Give _____ the strength to take care of his/her family and touch_____'s heart to appreciate his/her stylists or barbers. Teach_____ how to deal with problems in a timely manner and to be honest. Bless _____ with good health and allow him/her to prosper even as his/her soul prospers. Bless_____ to be good to his/her employees by giving vacation or sick leave, with no booth fee, because you said in Proverbs 3:27, "Withhold not good from them to whom it is due, when it is in the power of thine hands to do it."

5

Seeds of Wisdom for Our Co-workers

I have worked with and been associated with many stylists and barbers. I realized that I had to stop merely going to church and truly submit my life to Christ, in order to make it in this business. God allowed me to work around sisters and brothers who acted ugly, were selfish, jealous, vindictive, and just plain dirty. I thank God for every test, because it helped me to develop more fruit of the spirit (Gal. 6:9).

Some of you have experienced or will experience what I am about to mention. I've had stylists hold dryers for one another and also try to take my customers. When I wasn't in, they wouldn't give customers messages or a number to call me. They would lie and say I wasn't in when I was, use my products without permission, and talk about me to their customers. So I tell you this to you keep your eyes on God, because "no weapon formed against you will prosper," (Isa. 54:17). It's not the person, but the spirit behind the person trying to hurt you. If you have a few customers, stay faithful because God promises if you are faithful over the few, He'll make you ruler over many (Matt. 25:21).

Don't make the mistake of comparing your business with another stylist or barber's. Why? First, you will always find someone who seems better than you, and discouragement will set in. Secondly, there will always be someone who doesn't seem as effective as you, and you will get puffed up with pride.

Let's deal with envy and jealousy. God warns us that where there is envy and jealousy, there is evil work. You may say, "I'm not jealous of anyone!" But check to see if there are areas where you always have something negative to say that might reveal the source of your jealousy. If you know someone with a lot of customers, and you say in your heart, "I'm not working that hard for anyone, that's just ridiculous," you're jealous! Stylists and barbers, be considerate of your coworker's time and family when you want your hair done. Communicate with each other, because I have seen where the enemy used small incidents to cause strife. For example, accidentally hanging up on a customer when I was putting them on hold, forgetting to give a message, and not letting a customer know their stylist was coming in or when they were returning, even when I didn't know whose customer they were. Be careful when asking coworkers for change when they're busy, and if they don't have it, you borrow what you need but never give it back, but when they get it from you, you seem to remember and never give them all the change you borrowed. Also, if your coworker is nice enough to allow you to use their product at least replace it where you go pick up supplies.

Some of us will forget about an appointment, but won't

admit it. Instead, we get upset with another stylist. Stylists and barbers, be mindful. Most other stylists are not out to cause you to lose money. But some things happen by mistake, we are all human. Stop being lazy and go educate yourselves by going to hair shows, coloring and cutting classes, and doing whatever you have to do to take your business to the next level. What it takes for one stylist may not be what it takes for you. It's time to stop talking and do something. If you're satisfied with your business, don't discourage others in the salon when they go out to further their business.

Proverbs 14:23 says, "In all their labor there is profit, but idle talk leads to poverty." Stop being jealous of your coworkers when you just want to take off all the time, eat, sleep, and have fun, because in Proverbs 10:23, it says, "Love not sleep, lest thou come to poverty; open thine eyes and thou shalt be satisfied with bread." Get a mentor that you can learn from in your salon or somewhere else. Barbers find a master barber that's willing to help you. If you're not confident about doing a particular style or cut, refer the client to someone else or ask the customer if they mind if another stylist performs that part of the service. Work as a team. Please don't expect that stylist to do it all the time. Buy tapes to learn what you need. I've learned people can hinder your growth by helping you all the time.

Some of us should be ashamed at how we just throw people's hair together and don't take pride in what we do. Some of the styles we know are not worth what you charged, and you wouldn't want to wear it yourself. If you wonder why your clientele won't grow, check yourself. It's very important that we take care of our oral and personal hygiene and wear clean uniforms and nice shoes. Avoid talking on cell phones while servicing clients. Make sure you don't expose your upper anatomy and underarm hair follicles while rendering services. Be careful coming to work smelling like your extracurricular activity(alcohol, smoking, sex) to name a few because before a client tells you they just won't come back.

Stylists and barbers, don't cause strife in the salon when you're trying to do things to make the salon better. Gossiping among your click only changes the atmosphere and causes confusion. If you don't want to participate in something, just don't; but remember, God blesses unity. If you have an issue with a salon guideline, let the owner know. Maybe it can be corrected. He hates those that cause "discord among the brethren," (Prov.6:19). God has shown me how the person that is behind all the confusion is normally the first one to get out; but that is how the enemy works, because he can keep working when he's not exposed. Let your coworkers know when they're doing good work by telling them how great it looks, and let the client know as well. You should encourage each other as often as possible. Now I must warn you, you will not be able to do this if you have jealously or envy in your heart. It must be done with sincerity. Also, be honest with your coworker in private when he or she is sending out work that does not represent the salon or them, because customers will spread the word. Remember, the truth will set you free.

Stylist and barbers that have been in the industry a while and your finances are suffering and I hear you all say "I need to rebuild my clientele "The Lord gave me a word for you "you don't need to rebuild, you need to change your attitude, be on time for clients and stop mistreating and abusing your clients and he will restore you." So many of you all clients Love you and miss you but they can't tolerate your behavior. The Lord said" If you would make the changes, he will restore your clients, booth renters". Some of you need to apologize and ask for forgiveness because you've sown some bad seeds in the industry with customers / product distributor. You've talked about your clients to other clients, there friends, and even there family members and you keep saying rebuild, "NO" do the right thing and be professional and run a business and not just do hair. It's easy to do hair but its harder to build a real consistent clientele without any business ethics. Ask yourself how would you feel if you had to wait an extra hour, with no phone call and this happens all the time. All of its not the devil some of you are just saying "Go somewhere else" and guess what? The clients will get some sense and go. I have to be honest to help you. We got to do better, this is a great industry.

Professional who have been in the business for years, please take a look back as to where you have come from and help the newcomers. Be sensitive, because there was a time when you only made money from booth rental, barely had gas money, no lunch money, not enough money to buy products, had to borrow products, or came to work with man/woman problems and didn't know how to deal with it. So help them and show them the way. If you live an alternative lifestyle, it's unfair for others to have to hear about your bedside manners as well. Treat others the way you want to be treated. Everyone deserves respect.

Try to treat each other with as much love as possible and convey a sense of humor. "Pursue the things which make for peace and the things by which one may edify another," (Rom. 14:19). We're all in this business, because we love hair, making people look great, and to make a good income.

Professionals you don't have to go out with your co-workers but you do have to walk in love with them. Be kind, speak when you come in and at least let them know you're gone. A lot of us profess to be Christians so walk in the LOVE of God and not just with your friends and church members.

Professionals, you also need to check your heart when you go on vacation or sick leave and won't recommend your clients to someone in your workplace because you feel that no one is good enough. You've sneakily talked about your co-workers to your clients so they rather not get in their styling chair. You lift your work and hair care above others but be aware there is still someone better than you and if something happens to you too long those same clients will find someone and if you leave the salon they will go to the stylist that you talked about and doesn't make all there clients look the same. So be careful what you be saying over the clients and about your co-workers because people can discern and see as well. Remember in Luke 14:11 Those who exalt themselves shall be brought low and those who humble themselves shall be exalted.

Stylist and barbers you need to get a heart check that when you go out sick or on vacation that you deliberately don't refer or suggest for your clients to come to anyone at your salon/workplace. God sees your heart. It's sad, that when you do you send them, you send your client to someone that's not as good as you, so you can look great and have something negative to say. Yet on purpose you don't send them to the ones that you know can satisfy them and they get more compliments or be asked "who did your hair" cause that will hurt your pride. Plus you suppose to be a Christian but you've talked about your co-workers behind their backs to your customers to make yourself look like you the only one do good hair and use good products, that they don't want to come when you out. It's funny that you never see that all your clients look the same , Wow but you such a great stylist. Stylist / barbers leave that salon and some of your clients just waiting to try a new look from the stylist you talked about so bad and called them unprofessional as if you were born with a gold spoon in your mouth. I have to help you before you get too lifted up in pride. God said in Matthew 23:12 whosoever that exalts himself shall be humbled(brought low), and whosoever humbles himself shall be exalted.

Please stylist and barbers stop being loud and argumentative with your co-workers in front of the client, it gives the salon a negative imagine and having clients leave with a negative experience. Watch your tone in the salon and stay out of other stylist and their client conversation it only causes confusion. And some of you wonder why your business never grow. I can tell you why "It's You"

We're all guilty of gossiping at one point, we will not say it but agree with the person. You got to have some tough skin in the industry and know who you are in Christ. For example, I like wearing my hair pulled back when working to be comfortable and I hear clients talk about me to their stylist (co-worker) and say "I'm glad my stylist keeps her hair done." and instead of the stylist lifting me up by saying "she keeps that pretty hair up", she would say "I know Honey" and hearing it hurts but you have to go on or its sad. Clients would say "how she getting those clients out so fast?" instead of saying "it's the anointing and God blessed her with that speed and she loves what she does", the stylist would say "The hair not properly drying or she's using inexpensive products which wasn't true. Yes my flesh wanted to tell her off, but the spirit of God said "No she gonna go through a drought for putting her mouth on you and you will have to pray her through that season, whether she knows it or not." Yes, it happened and I prayed for her until I saw the season change. Be careful what you say about others and especially your co-workers that you profess to care about.

Before you talk about your coworker performance to others, give suggestion and help him/her we all started out somewhere. If it wasn't for God grace some of us wouldn't have made it in the industry. Your negative words will come back to bite you in the butt. What about all the clients that gave you a chance? How easily we forget.

Notes

What things can I do to improve relations at my workplace and with my salon owner?

_____

_____

_____

_____

_____

_____

_____

_____

_____

_____

_____

_____

_____

_____

_____

_____

_____

_____

_____

_____

_____

_____

_____

Daily Confessions to Enjoy Your Coworkers

I will enjoy my coworkers today regardless of their mood. This is the day the Lord has made, and I will rejoice and be glad in it (Psalms 118:24). I will not envy or be jealous of my coworkers, because God said he is no respecter of person. If you bless them, you will bless me. I will not criticize my coworkers. If I have a problem, I will go to them as the Holy Spirit directs me. I will love them with the love of the Lord regardless of how they act. I will pray for them, their family, and their businesses. I will keep a positive attitude no matter what I'm going through. When things get heavy, I will pray and praise, without getting the wrong attitude and hurting the people around me. Heavenly Father, bless my coworker's business to prosper. The joy of the Lord is my strength (Neh. 8:10), because happiness depends not on what happens to me on the outside, but joy that comes from knowing God.

6

Customer survey

I personally conducted a survey with customers at work, so that this manual wouldn't just be my thoughts and experiences in the salon. Below are the major complaints received from customers about their stylist or barber. I know customers may be the problem sometimes, but please study the results and make changes as needed. Some of these even hit me in the face:

1. Overbooking. Having customers sit for hours before they are serviced, especially when they have scheduled appointments. It's wrong to book 4 and 5 clits at the same time knowing you can't do all of them in a timely manner. It's wrong to fill up all the dryers and be inconsiderate of your co-workers. You all make excuses for having your clients at the salon 4 to 8 hours when you need to see that you are OVERBOOKING! Run a business and stop just doing hair it's not fair to the clients and to your coworkers that have to hear the complaining while you ignore it.

2. Not being on time. You tell a customer to be in at nine, and you show up at ten.
3. Eating while rendering services to the client.
4. Gossiping. Talking too much instead of working.
5. Family members and close friends who pay tend to be overlooked and kept in the salon for extremely long periods of time. We tend to think they have nothing better to do, so they go elsewhere and you don't understand why. One family member may ask you something about another family member; but when it gets back to them, it was turned around, and your family leaves and you don't know why.
6. Asking customers to pick up supplies and food for you all the time.
7. Not returning clients' phone calls or pages in a timely manner.
8. Not listening to their complaints. Try to rectify your mistake by giving them a discount or free hairdo, especially when you know deep inside that you messed up.
9. Giving the customer what you want them to have instead of what they want.
10. Servicing area is filthy and unkempt.
11. Not treating customer's hair with the proper conditioners, or when they ask, you are reluctant to tell them what product you're using. Stylists seem especially reluctant to tell the customer what hair color they're using. Post your changes for your business or pass out notices, than being rude to your clients when you tell them.

12. Having your children or family at salon while working bothers other stylists and customers. Let clients know that you are running behind, it's just being courteous and giving good customer service. Give them a time to return in case they have something to do than have them wait for hours. Some of you have the audacity to talk crazy when a client has a legitimate complaint or has to be at work. Come on stylist and barbers start scheduling properly. Most of our clients are not self-employed so they have to be on time for work and we should honor that and not have them stressed trying to get there. If you can't get them out on time be honest and give them your next availability and stop just trying to make their money.

13. Use of profanity and unclean talk by barbers, stylists, and customers.

14. Doing each other's hair while paying clients are waiting

15. Going outside to smoke while client is waiting to be serviced.

16. Allowing other customers to talk loudly and use profanity in the salon or clients talking so loudly on their cell phones that it disturbs others.

17. Coming to work smelling like cigarettes, alcohol, etc.

18. Not being consistent in your pricing.

19. Talking about your coworkers or personal problems all the time.

20. Workers taking up all the parking spaces and causing clients to have to walk further or find a parking space. You will be at work all day or for hours, so don't be so selfish.

21. Sanitize your hands at all times. especially coming out the restroom. I wash them in there and sanitize them for the client to see. Don't touch the garbage cans or other items before touching clients heads, they will be watching.

22. Don't eat over your clients head, especially while styling them, that is horrible.

23. Stop telling customers to come on to the salon knowing you have told 5 other clients the same thing. How would you feel if someone did you that way. You will reap it back along life journey.

7

Handling offenses

Offense. A major hindrance (unresolved bitterness, resentment, and unforgiveness in a broken relationship) grieves the Holy Spirit and undermines unity in prayer, which is vital to revival.

Offend. To cause dislike, anger, or vexation; cause hurt feelings or deep resentment; not an intentional hurting, but it may indicate merely a violation of the action senses of what is proper or fitting; deliberate rudeness, insult, or contemptuous indifference to courtesy.

As stylists and barbers, we have to handle everything in a professional manner and with the love of God to avoid offending our clients. I had to really ask God to help me with this spirit of offense. I couldn't understand how a client could come in an hour late and not expect you to say anything. And even when you do say something politely, they still get mad. I advise you to reschedule them or let them know you will have to work them in, because it not fair for the other scheduled clients to have to wait. Yes, things do happen and clients will run late, but it constantly happens and by coincidence, it may be the same client having to wait or a new client—and that leaves a bad impression, and they sometimes won't return. Watch out for this, because the enemy will do things to rob from you; he's slick. Communicate with the client if they are open to changing their time or day, and be mindful when scheduling. Look over your book some time and pray, and God will show it to you.

Stylists and barbers, God warns us that offenses will come in life. Jesus, being the son of God, offended many. So we know we will offend someone, but it should only be for the Word, and not because we have a nasty attitude or problem. That is why He warned the disciples in Luke 17:1 that it is impossible for no offenses should come. In Psalm 119:165, He also gave us great insight into people who really love God. "Great peace has they which love thy law: and nothing shall offend them." So I encourage you to be careful on how you handle matters. Oftentimes I was right, but the way I responded was simply wrong. James warns us in 1:19, "Let every man be quick to hear, slow to speak, and slow to take offense and get angry." This was a challenge for me, but I make an effort now to try and not get offended, especially when I've tried hard to satisfy my client.

For example, a customer arrives late for an appointment and tells me, "You're taking too long." I would respond, "You weren't on time." That only offended them more. Another example, a customer writes a bad check, and you add a returned check fee. The customer asks, "Why are you charging me a fee?" I would say, "It's the same thing everyone else does, and you don't say anything." That was the wrong response. I would even be harsh on the phone when they called to cancel, until my sister-in-law told me to smile when

I talk, and my voice would become more pleasant. I never wanted to be mean. Now some of my customers call and say, "Are you smiling?" Try it. It works.

The Bible warns us in Proverbs 18:19, "A brother offended is harder to be won over than a strong city, and contentions separate them like the bar of a castle." I learned this after losing some good, faithful customers. Don't get me wrong, some people are going to get offended regardless of how nice you are, because they have a spirit of offense and don't want any correction when they're wrong. Be kind, be gentle, and tell the truth in love. Because if you don't, you will have to go to the person to have the peace of God. Matthew 5:23 says, "bring thy gift to the altar, and there remember that thy hath ought (offense) against thee: Leave thy gift before the altar; and go thy way; first be reconciled to thy brother, and then come offer the gift." We know when we have offended a client; we have to be quick to get it right.

Here are a few things you can do in this business to avoid unnecessary offenses:

1. Don't allow customers to pay you what they want you to have, because the day you decide to charge them the actual price, they'll get offended. Charge all customers the same; only give discounts on birthdays or customer appreciation day to alleviate problems. Customers talk amongst themselves.
2. Post your return check fee where it is visible.
3. Let the customer know the price of any complimentary service.

4. Let your customers know ahead of time when you plan to take time off.

5. Season your words with salt that you might know how to answer any man.

6. Stay calm, be kind, and speak the truth when clients are short with you or become offended with you. "Let your speech be always with grace, seasoned with salt, that ye may know how ye ought to answer every man." (Col. 4:6).

7. Let your friends and family know you can't afford to keep doing their hair and not get paid. You are trying to stay in business and not get burned out, because it will if you keep doing hair for free.

8. When you accept their business, inform call-ins and walk-ins when you will be working them in, even if you don't have a customer the moment they arrive. This way, they will understand they might not be able to get right in and out.

9. Ask for a twenty-four-hour cancellation notice when possible. At the very least, ask customers to call ahead if they must break appointments at the last minute. Be careful with text messaging as your main source of communication. This is a people business, and communicating on the telephone will help avoid many problems and help you build client-business relationship. Texting can sometimes create a problem because people tend to forget that phones are not humans and don't have emotions. Clients will read more into it sometimes or you may just schedule them

wrong if you misread. Clients will send messages back to back, and it can throw you off sometimes.

10. Let your co worker know in love you don't want to be bothered or want them in your space, instead of offending them by being mean and rude in front of your clients. If they have a question about helping them or need help let them know in Love by whispering in their ear "not today or I don't have time." Because you're going to reap bad things from being mean to people on purpose.

11. Let clients know that you are running behind, its just being courteous and giving good customer service. Give them a time to return in case they have something to do than have them wait for hours. Some of you have the adacity to talk crazy when a client has a legitimate complaint or has to be at work. Come on stylist and barbers start scheduling properly. Most of our clients are not self-employed so they have to be on time for work and we should honor that and not have them stressed trying to get there. If you can't get them out on time be honest and give them your next availability and stop just trying to make their money.

12. If you're tired or overbook don't take anymore clients because the client can tell by your spirit when it's not right you may half shampoo or not style as normal. The client you think is so sweet and loves you so much will be the one get offended and leave you and take others with them.

13. It's wrong to overbook and take of all the dryers from your co-workers, stop being so selfish

14. Please don't talk to co-worker over client while at shampoo bowl, Most clients love this time. so if you have an emergency and need something pull your co-worker to the side. Clients be listening and forming there own opinion of you, especially if you talking about someone. And some of your co-workers will talk about you soon as you leave the area with their client.

15. Stop allowing your clients to control the atmosphere of the salon. Clients want to relax and enjoy their visit. Some of you just love a lot of mess and noise. Ask the holy spirit to help you. this is a job not a hang out. You will run other people clients away or they will change days to avoid being there when it's loud and messy. Or hurry up and get your own place and run it like a zoo.

16. It's rude to be on your blue tooth the whole time while over a clients head, regardless of who it is, you are at work .Clients will get offended so apologize and take care of the client,

17. To the Religious stylist/barber I love God too with all my heart, but clients don't want you praying and preaching while you have them waiting. God knows you have a job to do and there a time and place for everything.

8

Prayer for your hands

Did you realize we can pray for our hands? My personal research revealed that God used the word hands 527 times in the Bible. This lets me know they are important to Him. Our hands are used to worship God, give, express our feelings, prosper, eat, help others, work, take care of personal hygiene, heal, and much more.

Close your eyes for two minutes and try to imagine life without your hands. Learn to appreciate how blessed our hands are. They are used to help people look and feel better about themselves.

Read the following Scriptures. God warns us of the blessings and curses that can be on our hands:

> "The Lord has blessed you in all the works of your hands." (Deut. 2:7)
> "The Lord your God will bless you in all your harvest and in the work of all your hands, and your joy will be complete." (Deut. 16:15)
> "The Lord will open the heavens, the storehouse of His bounty, to send rain on your

land to bless all the works of your hands (that is, if you pay attention to His commands)." (Deut. 28:12)

"If you don't pay attention to His commands, the Lord will send curses, confusion, and rebuke you in everything you put your hands to, until you are destroyed and come to sudden ruin because of the evil you have done in forsaking Him." (Deut. 28:15)

"He thwarts the plan of the crafty, so that their hands achieve no success." (Job 5:12)

"The Lord is known by His justice, the wicked are snared by the work of their hands." (Ps. 9:16)

"May the favor of the Lord our God rest upon us; establish the work of our hands for us—yes, establish the work of our hands." (Ps. 90:17)

"A little sleep, a little slumber, a little folding of the hands to rest—and poverty will come on you like a bandit and scarcity like an armed man." (Prov. 6:10)

"Lazy hands make a man poor; but diligent hands bring wealth." (Prov. 10:4)

"From the fruit of the lips a man is filled with good things, as surely as the works of his hands reward him." (Prov. 12:14)

"Diligent hands will rule; but laziness ends in slave labor." (Prov. 12:24)

"The fool folds his hands and ruins himself."
(Ecc. 4:5)

"Two are better than one, because they have
a good return for their work." (Ecc. 4:9)

I came to the conclusion that we must conduct our business
God's way. That means five primary things:

1. Stop being lazy.
2. Take time to properly condition and take care of the
   hair.
3. God will give you his supernatural ability to do great
   work.
4. Work together more, because God said, "Two are
   better than one" (Ecclesiastes 4:9). Give clients what
   they want; unless we know from our training and
   experience that it will be harmful to them.

9

Seeds of wisdom for New stylists and barbers

I want to write and encourage you not to give up on the industry. Everything has its negative aspects, but there are so many good things about your profession. I know it's hard not to get discouraged when the people you love won't support your new endeavor, but just keep going. Get a mentor; don't waste time around stylists/barbers that just talk and never try to impart something in your life to help your business. They will be growing while you stagnate. God warns us not to despise small beginnings; you may have only one or two customers to start off. Just keep being faithful and watch your business grow.

As new stylists and barbers, I must be honest with you, because I see a lot of students coming out making the following mistakes:

1. Don't just be a good hairstylist, learn about hair care.
2. Don't come into the industry assuming you know everything. There's always something to learn.

3. Don't try to build a clientele at the salon while still doing hair at home. Some customers won't follow you and pay your prices.

4. Don't expect to build a clientele when staying away from the workplace 80 percent of the time; it's not going to work. When you don't have any customers, hang around coworkers to learn and ask questions. God may send you some walk-ins due to your faithfulness.

5. Realize it takes time to grow a strong, basic clientele; it doesn't happen overnight. Accept that sometimes all you may make for a week is booth rental but be happy and faithful and that will pass too. I did it, and so can you.

6. Keep you appearance up, so people will want you as a stylist/barber.

7. Be excited about your profession.

8. Accept constructive criticism from others, to help you.

9. Stay encouraged, and don't get jealous of others. There are enough people in the world to build a clientele.

10. Don't compete with other stylist on social media. Let your work speak for itself. Word of mouth is powerful.

Remember, "The race is not given to the swift or the strong, but to the one that endured to the end" (Eccl. 9:12).

Stylists' and Barbers' Prayer

Heavenly Father, in the Name of Jesus, I thank you for my hands. Continue to anoint my hands to do the work that is given to me. Forgive me, if I've used my hands for anything that does not honor you. Father, I realize slow work does not always mean quality work; therefore, give me the speed I need to do timely and quality work. Father, bless me to financially bless the person who helps me. I won't take them for granted, because they are to enjoy the fruits of their labor also. You said in Your Word that you will bless all the works of my hands, not some.

God, I work expecting to satisfy every customer you allow my hands to touch. Father, I honor you and I praise you for these hands. Bless my hands to be a blessing to someone else in my workplace, home, family, neighborhood, or whoever you send my way. God, you told me in Ecclesiastes 9:10 that "whatever my hands find to do, do it with my might; for there is no work, or device, or knowledge, or wisdom in the grave where I am going."

So Lord, give me strength to do the things I need to do. Amen.

10

Seeds of Wisdom for Our Family

Due to the long hours at work, especially in African American salons, I must address the issue of our families. I would hate to see some of you make the same mistakes I made out of ignorance. In a few words, go home.

Time is something you can't get back. You can't make All the money in the world. While you're afraid to say no, the enemy of our souls (the devil) is saying yes to steal from you. God warns us not to give the devil a foothold. We do that by neglecting our families, parental duties, marriage duties, our parents, and our friendships by not giving them the time, help, and love they need because we are at work all the time. Most Caucasian salons have set hours, but many African American salons do not. Yes, thank God for the money, but God warns us in Proverbs 16:25, "There is a way that seemeth right unto a man, but the end is destruction." It may seem right to work two jobs and stay at the shop 24/7, but the end result is broken marriages, neglected kids, stress, health problems, depression, and lost friendships. Take time to go to your children's school, play a game with your child, take your mate to lunch, take a walk, visit a sick friend or family member, and attend a friend's wedding, bridal shower, or graduation, because you can't get these special moments back. Your customers will understand, but if you act like they are of no importance, so will your customers. If your customers don't realize you have a life, that's okay; God will give you customers that do. Trust God.

I worked in a prison for sixteen years, while doing hair part-time jobs with a full-time clientele, and I regret it to this day. I had to ask God to forgive me. It wasn't until my mother fell dead at fifty-seven from a stroke that I decided to listen to God. "God, I surrender and trust you with my business." To be honest, I didn't want to have to deal with people for my income. I enjoyed the paychecks and didn't have to put up with the mess from clients. I promise you, God will provide. I went full-time and made more money working fewer days, but I never thought it would be without my mom. I must admit, there are times that I cry and wish I had left the shop to go be with her.

I once went to a hair seminar where a stylist told us that her best friend ended up with her husband, and our mouths fell open. She told us it hurt, but after looking back, she saw how she neglected her marriage by not taking time off and not saying no to late customers. Some of us will say they were wrong, and they would have done it anyway. I don't know. That was her assessment. So I encourage you, married stylists and barbers, to take time for your mate's needs, even if that means being late or having to reschedule every now and then. I didn't say neglect clients, but take care of your business. The Bible says that a married woman is to take care of her husband's things. I wish someone had told me those years ago. Married barbers go home as well and stop hanging out with the single fellows. Your family misses you and needs you too. The purpose of getting client telephone numbers is so that you can call them when things come up. Just don't give out too much information. Make time for your family before it's too late.

I encourage you to stop neglecting your parental duties, because you make good money and people don't mind keeping your kids. Everybody needs a break. I've seen stylists, after completing their clients, go out to eat, go shopping, or talk with other stylists, instead of going home. This is so unfair. Don't take advantage of your caregivers. It's your job to raise the kids. I encourage you to stop putting off having children, getting married, taking a real vacation, going to a child's field trip, among other things. Trust God. He will provide for you and give you a clientele designed for your lifestyle. I know you love your family and you try to show them by doing their hair sometimes, but don't neglect your paying customers. Explain to your family that you are running a business, and you may have to do them when you have no paying customers. I've seen where stylists continue to do family's hair for free and get burned out because of no profit.

Stylists and barbers, show your family you appreciate and miss them when you're at the salon. They really don't know that sometimes we miss them so badly, we could cry. I remember when my husband and son would call me at the salon to check on me and would ask, "What are you doing?" Instead of expressing my heart, and saying, "I'm doing hair but missing you all," I'd say "Hair" in an ugly way. They both told me it hurt them, and they both stopped calling. I was too busy with a client to say, "Just thinking about you all and wish I was there." Now I wish they would call more. So be gentle and grateful that you have a family that loves you and misses you. Last but not least, let's not neglect our church family as well. I know you work hard on Friday and Saturday, but get energized like you are when you're making money to give honor and praise to God. Remember, he tells us in Hebrews 10:25, "Not forsaking the assembling of ourselves together, as the manner of some is; but exhorting one another: and so much the more as ye see the day approaching."

Some people will not go to church; you just do what's right. I know you're trying to be available, but people do what they want. I encourage you to honor God on the Sabbath and keep it holy. We work and are on time for our clients, then make all kinds of excuses for being late to church, not participating in activities, and not going to church on a regular basis. Yes, God knows. He said, "For where your treasure (money) is, there will your heart be also," (Matt. 6:21). Let's keep our priorities in order. I've learned now that God is first, then family, and then our careers. People didn't teach us properly, God loves family and wants us to take care of our family, not neglect them for our careers.

To the unmarried stylists and barbers, I encourage you to search your heart when it comes to the things of God. Do away all the excuses when it comes to giving, participating, and attending at the house of God. First Corinthians 7:32–34 reads:

> "But I would have you without carefulness.
> He that is unmarried careth for the things that

belong to the Lord, how he may please the Lord; but he that is married caret for the things that are of the world how he may please his wife. There is a difference between a wife and a virgin. The unmarried caret for the things of the Lord, that she may be holy both in body and in spirit; but she that is married caret for the things of the world, how she may please her husband."

God loves marriage and wants the single person to have no distraction in serving the Lord, until they get married. This is the Word, so don't get mad. Get it right, so you can be really blessed. Enjoy your family is all I'm saying. This is one of the main reasons we choose to be self- employed and set hours conducive to our lifestyles. Let's give all glory and honor to God.

Professionals, I love my family and friends too, but to run a successful business you have to keep it business. If you allow you family and friends to come in whenever they want and don't pay you properly you will get frustrated and angry. My mother was the only family member I didn't charge and she respected my business enough to come when it was best for me. Building a cliental not based not around your buddies will create a monetary reward because friends and family tend to get jealous when they see you being blessed where as outside clients will appreciate you and the service you give. I've seen stylist break and be so mean because they weren't getting paid properly or on time. Stop allowing partial payments or no payments because they will go to another stylist and expect the same thing and will be shocked to find out some stylist are running a business not just doing hair. I've seen where family/friends will barely pay their stylist or barbers and then go elsewhere and pay almost double for the same service. I'm not saying don't be good to your family, but be careful it can destroy your business.

Stylist and barbers if you going to hire family members I encourage you to keep it business. I hear people say you can't work with family. I have a niece that works with me and you have to treat them as a worker like everyone else and make them abide by the rules and regulation to avoid problems. The enemy will sometimes use the person you love to create problems but I've learned to just talk to your love one and let them know your expectations and if it's not the place for them let them find somewhere else. It was times I wanted to tell my niece to get out, but the Lord said "it's a mean world out there in these salons if you don't show her or walk in love with her until she grows in the industry she will self-destruct and real Love hides a multitude of Faults". She's building a good clientele and I do see changes and I know I will see greater changes. I'm happy because when her season is up at my salon she will be ready to handle anything and I'll be happy for her. So stay professional and run a business even with family.

11

Seeds of Wisdom for Our Finances

The last major topic I will discuss is finances. We should believe in God for our finances and walk in obedience by bringing our tithes and offerings to the store- house (church). God warns us in Malachi 3:10–11 that if we would give our tithes and offerings, He would stop the devourer from eating our seed, and our vine wouldn't cast its fruit before its time.

Many of you are operating under a curse and don't realize it. God warned the people by the Prophet Haggi, you bring home much but it seems like little. It's like a bag with a hole in it. God blows on it, because you don't honor his word and take care of the things of God. Excuses for not trusting God and not giving according to His Word are unacceptable to Him. God said in Isaiah 1:19, "if we're willing and obedient, we shall eat the good of the land." We can't expect this in our lives if we continue to lie, steal, cheat, gossip, fornicate, envy others, etc. We must discontinue shop-hopping and do right by the owners, who allow us to work in their salons. If you have left a salon out of order or used other stylists' products without their knowledge, I advise you to repent and make it right. I've learned that if you help someone else, God will bless you. Take your eyes off yourself and put them on someone else. For example, buy someone some supplies or a piece of equipment and see what happens. Ephesians 6:8 Knowing that whatsoever good thing any man doeth, the same shall he receive of the lord, whether he is bond or free. Also, if you have any areas of unforgiveness in your heart, ask God to help you. Pay your booth fee first; that's your responsibility, no matter how many clients you have. Your booking or you taking off have nothing to do with the owner. Stylists and barbers don't live in fear of charging what your services are worth. Our prices have to go up with the economy, product price increases, and according to the services you are rendering. If you never give yourself a raise, that is not your client's fault. All businesses get raises. Remember, you are running a business. You have taxes to pay, insurance, products, booth rental, health insurance, and etc. The enemy will speak to your mind and tell you that your customers will leave, but you must remember in 2 Timothy 1:7, "God has not given us a spirit of fear, but of love, power and a sound mind." We must trust God to take care of our customers and us. Surprisingly, when I made a five-dollar-price increase, because I haven't had it the year before, I had several regular customers leave. The Holy Spirit spoke and said, "Don't worry, God will supply all your needs." God sent me new customers who seemed to appreciate me, pay my prices, and even tip me and my shampoo tech. God is so awesome.

I worked with a barber that did amazing work. Being led by the Holy Spirit, I told him it was time to increase his prices. It took him a few years, but he did it and is more successful than ever. While working in two salons, I was shocked to see the stylists and barbers with fewer customers make more money than the ones with a lot. I didn't understand it until I got stuck in the same rut. I talked to God about it, and I found out that the stylists and barbers with fewer customers had confidence and were running a real business and making money, while the stylists and barbers with lots of customers were operating in fear and trying to have friendships, even though they were working so much harder. I learned people pay for what they want, especially if you're giving excellent service. Now don't take this out of context, I didn't say overcharge anyone.

I remember the season in the industry when I had so much debt that I couldn't even buy lunch, and no one knew but me, God, and a trusted person I had praying for me. I couldn't blame the devil or anyone else. I was living above my means, helping folks that weren't right, and I had to sow my way out. I had to be honest and tell my friends I couldn't do anymore baby showers or birthday clubs, because, for some reason, people feel hairstylist keep money. I wanted to file bankruptcy, but God said, "No, you must learn from this and get some self-control. It was hard for me, but I paid off a 40,000 debt. So I share this with you to help you and let you know that you can make it. I learned to say "No," and I say it with love. Some people invite you all to stuff just for your money, be smart and stop giving to everyone.

Get out of debt, because something is wrong in our finances when we drive nice cars and live in big homes, but put a raggedy cape on a customer and use messed-up towels to service your clients, or not enough towels. You can act like you have it together, but it shows that you don't when you're doing twenty-five heads a week and still borrowing from your coworker who is building a clientele. And it's sad when you borrow money from clients. I've seen stylist take all kinds of vacation, but it takes them forever to replace a piece of equipment they use on a regular basis. If you have to keep borrowing supplies give your coworker something for using their products or replace the items. We must be honest in this profession. I don't mind you borrowing supplies, but I don't like anyone to use my equipment that I work hard to get and keep up., especially when it's not cheap. Be honest with God and ask him to help you with your finances and priorities.

It reminds me of the story of the virgins preparing to meet the bridegroom in Matthew 25:1–13. Five virgins put oil in their lamps and five virgins didn't. At midnight when the bridegroom came, the five foolish virgins said to the five wise virgins, "Give us some of your oil; for our lamps have gone out." But the wise virgins answered, "Not so; lest there be not enough for us and you; but go ye rather to them that sell, and buy for yourselves." And when they went to buy oil, the bridegroom came, and they were left out. I know that sounds harsh, but it's not right to keep borrowing from others while you make money.

I once had a new customer, who called and asked for several things and then asked me for a discount after I told her the price. She then said, "Girl, you're a Christian." I said,

"Yes, I love God, and you do too, but "a laborer is also worthy of his hire," (Lk. 10:7). I'm not saying never give discounts, just be led by God in your business. All ground is not good soil. When this customer came in and received the services, she paid the price, apologized, and gave me a good tip. She said she was convicted in her spirit and that I deserved what I charged.

All stylists and barbers, please have a savings account. It's bad for us to be so blessed and not have a reserve to keep us going when bad weather comes. Customers have financial problems, pregnancy, family emergencies, or—God forbid—you should get sick. And in the African American community don't let 5 of your clients go natural due to the others are doing, won't admit they don't have money to come to salon or thinking it less affordable you will get discouraged. Trust me if you operate in integrity and good customer service you will be ok. We need to have a reserve, so we won't stress out when we have to take time off and cancel our appointments because of emergencies. I've seen stylist because they had to take off quit the salon and relocate their clients to avoid paying booth fee while they are out. You are leasing the space whether you are there or not. If you choose to work part time that's your decision not the owner. You have to be prepared for that loss of income. Invest in short term and long term disability if possible. I've seen customers go through financial hardship, and the first place they cut out of the budget is the salon or barber shop. The same customers will go to someone doing hair in their home, even if you offer them a discount until things get better. So be prepared and ask God for the wisdom to know what to do. You still have a responsibility to pay booth when you are out sick or take a leave of absence. I've seen stylist leave a place to avoid paying when their stuff was in that person place of business. It's not the salon owner's fault she has to keep things still going if you go out or not.

I promise, if you have savings for one or two months' regular expenditures, it will help you to feel better and less stressed. Know your seasons in the industry; January gets busy but normally slows down during the winter. In July and August, professionals don't spend a lot on products as families are vacationing, but business normally picks back up for school time. All of our seasons aren't the same; just learn yours, so you can be on top of it.

In Proverbs 3:10, it says, "Honor the Lord with thy substance, and with the first fruits of thine increase; so shall thy barns be filled with plenty (appointment book with customers), and thy presses shall burst with new wine (new clientele). Plant seeds of new customers in the earth, so you won't be dependent on certain customers. You will have a large client base. Remember, God takes pleasure in the prosperity of his servants (Ps. 35:27). Let's trust God with our finances, even when the economy goes haywire. Don't listen to the enemy of your soul (the devil) who will say you can't afford to tithe. He will tell you that when you have a shortage. Don't receive it and keep being faithful. Trust God and continue to do quality work with quality products, regardless of what others are doing around you or what other salons are doing. Some people are a disgrace to our profession, but people do what they do. You just do your best. Don't lower your standards; have confidence and know that God takes care of his children. Everybody is not looking for a shortcut, and they know quality verses quantity. I told the stylist in the salon that after 2014, there would be a shift in the industry; but great customer service will be the key. He promised us in Psalm 126:5 that "Those that sow in sorrow shall reap in joy."

Stylist and barbers, it's time for us to stop trying to impress others by going out to eat, shopping all the time, and hanging out with the coworkers after work for drinks when you know you can't afford it. Be honest with yourself and say no sometimes, bring your lunch, and get your finances in order. If you don't deal with your situation, it will deal with you. Stay faithful in you're giving, so you can claim the promises of God. You can't claim the promises and not apply the principles of tithing and offering. When you do it God's way, you can confess and reap the manifestation of God's will to supply all your needs. Remember, he said if you're willing and obedient, you shall eat the good of the land. If you keep thinking with a poverty mentality, you won't ever get the clients you desire, be able to pay booth rental properly, and buy good equipment and supplies. Get in the Word of God to renew your mind.

Don't be afraid to take credit cards; if you don't, you will be missing out on some increase. If clients don't have money, they will cancel; but if you accept credit cards, they may still come and charge the service. If you refuse to renew your mind in this area, it will be your loss, trust me. I told you all to report your income and pay taxes, because if you have never worked a job with taxes and don't have enough credits for social security, you won't be able to draw anything from SSI or disability. I met a stylist that had worked for thirty years. at a convention, who was sixty-five years old, and she encouraged all of us to report our income. She told me she lied about taxes her entire career as a stylist. She was taught to not to report what she was making, and was making plenty of now went to get her SSI, she found out she didn't qualify. She had no other income. Unfortunately, due to her husband's recent death, she will be able to draw his benefits. She asked me to stress this to everyone after purchasing my book. So do the right thing, prepare your profit-and-loss statements, and pay your estimated taxes. Last but not least, you need to start (if you haven't already) to help those in need in your community with your talent and financial resources. You can do that by giving free cuts/ styles to those less fortunate and giving to the homeless or to your local food bank, because God promised in Proverbs 19:17, "He that lendeth to the poor He shall repay." And there's nothing like it when God pays you.

Prayer for Finances

"You said you will supply all my needs according to your riches in glory, so I believe You for my booth rental, supplies, tools, and everything I need to run a professional business." (Phil. 4:19)

"The blessing of the Lord maketh rich and add no sorrow to it." (Prov.10:22)

"The liberal soul shall be made fat; and he that watereth shall be watered also himself."(Prov. 11:25)

"I'm out of debt, my needs are met; I got plenty more to put in store. For I am the head and not the tail. I'm blessed going in and I'm blessed going out. My children are blessed. The Lord is my Shepherd and I shall not want." (Ps. 23:1)

"My God is able to do exceedingly, abundantly, above all that I could ask or think, according to the power that worketh in me." (Eph. 3:20)

"I am a tither, and God, You said that if I give it shall be given unto me, good measure, pressed down, and shaken together and running over, men shall give unto my bosom. For with the same measure I meet withal it shall be measured to me again." (Lk. 6:38)

After confessing these scriptures, start being faithful to God and see him work in your business. He will send you clients that will pay you double, that will appreciate you, that will be faithful to you, that will respect your business, and you will have more than enough. He will bless you with enough to be a blessing to others. Trust God, and you won't go wrong. Hallelujah!

Stylist and barbers in Genesis 8:22 God said while the earth remainth, seedtime and harvest, and cold and heat, and summer and winter, and day and night shall not cease. So you have to learn your seasons in the business. The word shows us that even the ants know to store up for winter time. And we are higher than any insect so we should have the wisdom to know when the winter time comes, clients hair last longer, bad weather comes where you or your clients may not make it to the salon, and people tend to stay in more with family. So be smarter and save so you can still pay your booth rental and your regular bills without so much stress. Spend your money wisely and don't try and buy for everybody during the Holidays. Don't ever stop sowing money in good ground that way you will always have a harvest coming in. And when the harvest is ready be prepared to work, don't be lazy. Harvest time is not a time to sit back it's a time to gather in. Be at the salon and stop telling your co-workers to call you if someone calls or walk-ins, the enemy knows you not expecting nothing so you miss out. Stop saying "whats for me is for me", because that sounds good but it can be for you but if you not there and being slothful you can miss what was for you. You ever heard the saying the early bird gets the worm. Some of you sleep so much and expect to be successful, I hate to tell you your finances won't change until you change your way of running your business, clients need to know you are available. Proverbs 10:4-5 he becomes poor that dealth with a slack hand but the Hand of the diligent makes rich. He Who gathers in the summer is a wise person, but he who sleeps in harvest is a son who causes shame. That's the word professionals so get busy and enjoy the industry.

God said in John 3:16 he wished above all things that we prosper and be in good health as our souls prosper. He wants us to be blessed. He takes pleasure in the prosperity of his servants . Psalm 35:27 Just because no one taught you the true word of God doesn't make it not be true. A lot of stylist and barbers get caught up in gambling, playing the lotto, overcharging to make it over, but only make things worse for themselves. You've got to trust God with your finances, go to work, be professional and you can make all the money you need. Be grateful to God that you have the ability to be creative and earn an income. Do your clients hair with Love and your work will reflect it. God is a God of more than enough. I've been blessed to do thousands of customers head while in the industry and I've learned there's a difference. Customers come and go, some barely want to pay and want something for free, but clients don't mind paying for their services, will tip you and show you they appreciate you all year long. When you honor God with your finances, he will bless you with an awesome clientele, but you got to be faithful. Proverbs 28:20 A faithful person will be richly blessed. But one eager to get rich will not go unpunished. So God don't mind us having money because he knew it would help us take care of our families, but vehicles, homes, go to dentist, but medicine/vitamins, vacation, help our parents, to name a few. So it's not money that's evil it's the lack of it that causes people to rob, steal, kill, lie defraud others, sell drugs, prostitute, and many other things that populate our criminal justice system with good people that choose the wrong path. Remember God doesn't have a problem with us having money because we need it to establish his covenant in the earth, to get people saved and to be a blessing to others. Ecc. 10:10 A feast was made for laughter, wine maketh merry: but money answer all things. I pray that I've helped you with your finances some way. Proverbs 12:15 The ways of a fool seem right in his own eyes, but a wise man listens to counsel. Build a clientele so you can prosper and not just want customers. Please use the wisdom God has given me to give to you so you can be successful and not learn the hard way.

12

Know your worth

Worth the value of something measured by its qualities or by the esteem in which it is held, having a value as in money.

In the cosmetology industry, you can determine your worth if you have the passion, ability, and education. You set the bar. You can be a stylist or barber to the stars, makeup artists, educator, and platform artist, work in a mortuary, behind the chair, or a salon owner. I see so many people coming to the industry who are afraid to charge for their services. If you feel it's not worth it, I understand; but coming in and making our profession look bad, hurt. I encourage you to put some worth on your body, back, legs, arms, hands, and the work you perform. It's worth every penny. Trust me, time will show you—the time away from your family and children.

If you don't see how much you are worth, you won't be able to pay your taxes, invest for retirement, pay your booth rental, health insurance, dental insurance, get disability coverage, and buy quality products and equipment. I know a lot of newcomers start off by doing services at home, but please work on yourself when u get in a salon, because your clients will treat you like they did in your house and not respect the industry. It's your responsibility to change it if you weren't charging them and allowing them to come whenever. Don't send messages out through Facebook or any social media to your clients. Deal with them in a professional way. If they don't want to pay your prices, let them go where they desire; and if they do come, charge them what you services are worth.

I have the attitude that my work is worth every penny with me giving quality service in a timely matter and using quality products. I feel that every client that sits in my chair is a star. If I never do a person that society calls a superstar. I just may be servicing the next First Lady of the United States or the next president of Apple. So know that you are valuable, and your work is too! If you think cheap, you draw cheap people that want something for nothing. You think quality, and you get quality people that don't mind paying for what they get. I'm being honest, so I can help you be successful in this business. Remember, knowledge comes from the world, but wisdom comes from God.

Conclusion

I pray that this information has helped you. Please purchase additional copies and distribute them to as many hairstylists and barbers you know. I pray for everyone, who reads this material, that their business will prosper and be a great success. Always remember, God said in Jeremiah 29:11, "I know the thoughts I think toward you, thoughts of peace and not evil, to give you hope and an expected end." Praise God for all of your blessings, because He created us to praise Him.

I know I covered many negative areas of our industry; but if we continue to ignore problems, they will eventually destroy our business. Think about some of the advantages we have in our industry. It's awesome.

1. The opportunity to set our own hours.
2. We earn the income we desire.
3. Daily income.
4. We make people look their best and have an opportunity to minister to them.

Because so many problems arise in our profession (namely, hair loss and skin disorders), continuing education is vital. Always believe God for favor. The Word says, God will bless the righteous with favor, and He will surround you as with a shield (Ps. 5:12).

About the Author

Michelle R. Johnson is a born again Christian and a licensed cosmetologist in Southaven, MS. Michelle shares practical, first hand experience on how Barbers and Cosmetologist can apply the Word of God in the business and live victorious.

Under the leadership of Dr. Leo Holt and by the inspiration of the Holy Spirit, she wrote this manual, Seeds of Wisdom for Cosmetologist and Barbers and is looking forward to writing other books and material in this area.

MIchelle is a member of the Professional Beautican Association and the Tennessee Beautician Association.

Michelle can be reached at cellphone 901-299-1872 or home phone 901-398-9341 for purchases or speaking engagements. Her email address is godswordforstylist1@ yahoo.com . The book can be purchased also at authorhouse. com or www.michellejohnsonbook.com

Printed in the United States
By Bookmasters